OREGON
W I N E

OREGON
WINE

A DEEP-ROOTED HISTORY

SCOTT STURSA

AMERICAN PALATE

Published by American Palate
A Division of The History Press
Charleston, SC
www.historypress.com

Front cover, top, left to right: Richard Sommer, founder of HillCrest Winery. *Courtesy of Douglas County Museum*; Pinot noir in a Dundee vineyard. *Photo by the author*; Unidentified vineyardist in Jackson County, late 1800s. *SOHS #12777, courtesy of Southern Oregon Historical Society.*
Front cover, bottom: Namasté Vineyards, located in the hills north of the Van Duzer corridor, gets the full benefit of the cool Pacific wind. *Photo by the author.*
Back cover: The Reuter Farm, circa 1910. *Courtesy of Washington County Historical Society and Museum.*
Back cover, inset: Two early wines from The Eyrie. *Photo by the author*.

First published 2019

Manufactured in the United States

ISBN 9781467140539

Library of Congress Control Number: 2019932628

Notice: The information in this book is true and complete to the best of our knowledge. It is offered without guarantee on the part of the author or The History Press. The author and The History Press disclaim all liability in connection with the use of this book.

In Memoriam

Jean Jacques Mathiot
1804–1876

Jack Parker Myers
1924–2001

CONTENTS

ACKNOWLEDGEMENTS

Thank you to the staff at the Oregon State Archives, the Southern Oregon Historical Society, the Douglas County Museum, the Washington County Museum and the Missouri Historical Society. Thank you to all the Oregon winemakers and vineyardists, both current and retired, who shared their stories with me. A special thanks to Jason Lett, who was very generous with his time, information and materials.

Thank you to winery owners and managers who shared their time and information, in particular, Mike Kuenz of David Hill and Lonnie Wright of The Pines 1852.

Thank you to Craig Greenleaf for the detailed account of the land-use initiative of the 1970s.

Thank you to the Comini family for the use of the photograph of their ancestor Luigi Comini.

Thank you to Kent Mathiot for the copy of the Mathiot family history and the supplemental information about the family.

Thank you to Brenda Eggert and Helen Gillenwater of the Eggert family for their time, information and materials.

Thank you to Nathan Warren and Amanda Sever of Harris Bridge Vineyard for the marvelous photograph of their vineyard.

Thank you to Rich Schmidt and the staff of Nicholson Library at Linfield College, both for their direct assistance and for their incredible job of creating and enhancing the Oregon Wine History Archive.

And last but not least, thank you to my wife, Kathy, for her patience and forbearance.

INTRODUCTION

THE HOLY GRAIL

My own introduction to fine wine came in 1980, during my late twenties. It came in the form of a mid-range Bordeaux from the 1970 vintage. It wasn't a great wine, but was so much better than anything I'd had before. I suddenly found myself with a new interest. My next foray was into California Cabernet, and I liked these as well. The next step was purchasing a couple of books in order to improve my knowledge of wine. One of these listed the four "noble" varieties, these being Cabernet Sauvignon, Pinot noir, Chardonnay and Riesling. I purchased a Pinot, one from a California winery whose Cabernet I liked, but it wasn't very good. I tried several more, with similar results. I tried several Burgundies, all priced in my comfort zone, and didn't like these either. I finally paid the premium for a bottle of 1972 Joseph Drouhin Chambertin-Clos de Bèze—again, not a great wine but so much better than what I'd already tried that I was willing to believe that there might be something to Pinot noir after all. I spent the 1980s on a quest to find Pinot both good and affordable. I eventually found a number from California that I liked; these were from cooler areas, such as the Carneros Hills just north of San Francisco Bay.

My experience was hardly unique. There were plenty of wine lovers seeking decent (and affordable) Pinot noir and plenty of California wineries trying to make it. Pinot noir was something of a holy grail for consumers and producers alike, and finding the better ones required persistence (as did making it).

I'd heard that there was good Pinot coming out of Oregon, but none of the wine stores in Tallahassee had any. That ended around 1988 or '89, when a newer store (Market Square Liquors and Wines) announced it would start carrying some and was holding a tasting to introduce them. I recall liking most of the wines but don't recall what they all were. The one I do remember was the 1985 Adelsheim, because I took two bottles home with me.

Over the course of the 1990s, I bought progressively more Oregon Pinot, which was not only better than its California competition but usually less expensive as well. I came to appreciate what I think of as the "Oregon style" of Pinot: lighter, more delicate, with red fruit (raspberry, strawberry) dominating. I still bought the occasional California Pinot; ironically, one of my most memorable wines of the period was actually from California, this being the 1991 Kistler "Catherine Cuvee," which was more Oregon in character than California.

My wife and I moved to Oregon at the beginning of 2007, and since then, our only Pinot purchases have been from our new home state.

LIFE IS TOO SHORT TO DRINK BAD WINE

A mantra of mine, I have it on a T-shirt, a ceramic coaster and a refrigerator magnet. There is a variation of it, "Life is too short to drink cheap wine," to which I do *not* subscribe. The correlation between price and quality is well short of 1.0, and with a little effort, one can find good wine that does not bust one's budget, so why bother to drink the bad stuff? If I find myself in a low-end eatery that has only generic whites and reds, I'll order beer (unless it's light beer, in which case I'll drink water). To some degree, this bias affects my beliefs about how much wine was made in Oregon during the early 1800s; the raw material available (wild berries, table grapes and native American grapes) made mediocre wine at best, and I want to believe that most people would have preferred hard apple cider or beer. I must remind myself, however, that vast quantities of bottom shelf wine are sold in this country (by the bottle, bag and box), and it might be that a French Canadian settler of the 1840s was perfectly happy with his blackberry wine. It's something to keep in mind while reading chapter 2.

DECONSTRUCTING MYTH

Anyone who's read books about Oregon wine knows that they usually include a half-to-full-page history of pre-1961 winemaking in the state. These accounts are nearly identical, because for the last forty years, authors have been simply repeating what others have written. As I began to research this book, it became obvious that nearly all of this information is not supported by historical record. I've identified the most frequently cited non-facts and tagged them as MYTHS OF OREGON WINEMAKING, and these are dealt with over the course of the book.

"THE BIRTHPLACE OF OREGON PINOT NOIR"

A contentious claim, one which has (I'm told) even triggered threats of lawsuits. It's nonsense. Pinot noir has only one "birthplace," that being somewhere in what is today the eastern part of France, and it took place two thousand years before Oregon even existed. The phrase is, in fact, a confounding of two entirely different events, the first being Pinot's first planting in the state and the second being the genesis of what I call the "Oregon Pinot noir phenomenon." The latter is the extraordinary rise of the Pinot-centric Oregon wine industry, a synergy between Willamette grapes that can make a wine rivaling the best of Burgundy and those who understood both how to make that wine and how to create and safeguard an industry. The information presented in this book shows that there is no relationship between the two events, with the first one (who first planted it) being essentially trivia, and the second one (the genesis of the Oregon Pinot noir phenomenon) meriting historical analysis.

A SPECIAL THANKS

Too important to be relegated to only the acknowledgements section (which almost no one ever reads) is my gratitude to Rich Schmidt, director of archives and resource sharing at Nicholson Library, Linfield College, McMinnville. Rich manages the Oregon Wine History Archive and has been an invaluable contributor of information and materials used in creating this work. Thank you, Rich; I'm hoping that by the time this book hits the store shelves, I'll have made good on my promise to buy you lunch.

Scott Stursa
November 17, 2018

1
THE VINE, PART I

The vine lived in northern France, probably in the Champagne district. It had been growing there for a long time, possibly for over one hundred years. It was surrounded by other vines of the same kind, all staked and carefully tended by their owners.

The vine was a peculiar variety known as *Pinot Meunier*. It's long been recognized as a close relative of Pinot noir but easily distinguished from that variety by its leaves, which appear to be dusted with flour (*Meunier* is the French word for miller), and the undersides of which are usually covered with a fine white down. Its grape has higher acid levels than Pinot noir, and that, along with its flavors and aromatics, has made it popular with Champagne producers. Nearly all Champagne contains Pinot Meunier, blended with Pinot noir and Chardonnay (the exception being *blanc de blanc*, which is usually made from Chardonnay). There are even Champagnes that are 100 percent Pinot Meunier.

Modern geneticists have determined Pinot Meunier to be a chimeric mutation of Pinot noir, essentially a plant within a plant. Extracting cells from the inner part of the vine and generating a plant from these results in Pinot noir; plants generated from the outer layer are dwarfed and unable to flower.

Like all cultivated grapevines, the vine was pruned in late winter, usually in February. In some years, the cuttings were simply discarded, but occasionally they were used to start new vines, either by the vineyard owner or by someone who purchased them. Sometime in the mid-1850s, cuttings from the vine were sent to a faraway place known as *California*.

The vine endured for several more years, but in the late 1860s, the root louse *phylloxera* swept through European vineyards. Probably introduced by plantings of the American species *Vitis labrusca*, the parasite destroyed millions of European vines; only after viticulturalists adopted the technique of grafting their native *Vitis vinifera* onto resistant roots were the vineyards successfully replanted.

But the vine perished. Like the thousands of vines surrounding it, it withered and died.

2

THE MAGIC LAND

Those colonizing the eastern shores of North America brought with them the crops with which they were familiar, and most of these grew well in the new land. Wheat, barley and rye all flourished, as did various fruits, such as apples, pears and plums. The notable exception was the European grapevine, *Vitis vinifera*. When planted in eastern North America, cuttings would root, grow for a few years, then sicken and die.

American efforts to cultivate *vinifera* began in the early 1600s at the Jamestown colony. These failed not so much because of diseases endemic to the eastern part of the continent (various fungal blights and phylloxera) but because there was no local enthusiasm for the project. Eventually, however, even those genuinely committed to viticulture realized *vinifera* was not a viable option and turned to native species.

The most common of these is *Vitis labrusca*, which ranges from Nova Scotia south to Georgia and west to the Mississippi River. The grapes of this species contain a high percentage of methyl anthranilate, a compound that gives them a distinctive flavor inexplicably described as "foxy." (Philip Wagner, one of the more influential American viticulturists of the mid-twentieth century, wrote, "I have been at some pains to sniff the 'effluvia' of several kinds of fox, in a number of celebrated zoos, and have been unable to detect the faintest resemblance.")[1] The best-known variety of *labrusca* is Concord, which makes great jelly and juice but awful wine; *labrusca* varieties used for wine are considerably subtler.

Vitis aestivalis, the "summer grape" (ripens in August), has a more southerly range, from Maine to Florida and west to Oklahoma. It is a tasty grape; the author would pick these from wild vines when he lived in north Florida. Many believe the Norton variety is the best native grape for red wine.

The native grape with the widest geographical range is *Vitis riparia.* Cold-tolerant and having a high degree of resistance to phylloxera, *riparia* and hybrids derived from it provide rootstock onto which *vinifera* is grafted.

Similar is *Vitis rupestris,* which, unlike most species of grape, grows as a shrub rather than a vine. It too is used to provide resistant rootstock and for creation of hybrid varieties.

In the far west, we find *Vitis californica,* which ranges into southwest Oregon. *Californica* is not a sweet grape; anyone wanting to make wine or jelly from it needs to add a lot of sugar.

All of the aforementioned can hybridize with *vinifera,* but one that cannot is the southern grape, *Vitis rotundifolia* (commonly called "muscadine"). It's a very different sort of vine, with thick-skinned grapes in loose clusters rather than tight bunches. It has its own sort of "foxiness," but despite this, a sweet wine named "Virginia Dare" (made from the Scuppernong variety) was the most popular wine in the United States prior to Prohibition.

These native American grapes can make an acceptable "everyday" sort of wine but have never made anything that approaches wine made from the better varieties of *Vitis vinifera.* But for Americans who wanted to make wine, it was the only option. Two hundred years of experience had led, by the early 1800s, to an inescapable conclusion: *vinifera* could not grow in North America. No one could explain why.

Except, it was, for equally inexplicable reasons, growing successfully on the other side of the continent. Spanish missionaries had been working their way up the California coast since the mid-1700s, building missions, saving souls and planting vines. The variety they were planting was called the "Mission," a sturdy, almost indestructible vine whose grapes made a dull but drinkable red table wine and a decent white fortified dessert wine. As it had been around since the 1500s, no one could recall its original name or point of origin, but modern geneticists have matched its DNA with a Spanish grape known as Listan Prieto. Prieto is a dark-skinned variant of a white grape used in sherry, which is probably why it does better as a dessert wine than as a dry one.

The last and northernmost of these missions was Mission San Francisco Solano, established in 1823 in what is today Sonoma County. By this time, the Mission grape was planted throughout the settled parts of central and southern California.

It was the following year that the British Hudson's Bay Company established Fort Vancouver on the north shore of the Columbia River. HBC wanted the colony to be self-sufficient and sent seeds for various grain and vegetable crops. By 1829, manager John McLoughlin was able to report a harvest of 1,500 bushels of wheat, 600 bushels of peas, 400 of barley, 300 of "Indian corn" and 7,000 of potatoes.[2]

Here we encounter MYTH NUMBER ONE: "The Hudson's Bay Company planted a vineyard at Fort Vancouver during the 1820s, using vines brought by ship from England. The vineyard allowed the company to produce its own wine rather than relying on imports."

The author has read numerous reports made by visitors to Fort Vancouver during the 1824–48 period, and not one mentions a vineyard. There also were numerous maps and illustrations made of the fort and surrounding grounds, and it isn't until 1854 that anything resembling a vineyard appears (*Merriam-Webster* defines a *vineyard* as merely "a planting of grapevines," but most people, when they hear the word *vineyard*, envision an expanse of land planted with multiple rows of vines). As for the vines being shipped from England, it took the better part of a year for a ship of the era to reach Fort Vancouver, and it's questionable whether vine cuttings could survive that long. Finally, the employees of HBC (at least those at the management level) were, in fact, drinking imported wine. An 1839 dinner-party guest of John McLoughlin's reported "decanters of various-colored Italian wines."[3]

There were *Vitis vinifera* vines growing at Fort Vancouver, just not in any quantity. The origin story of these vines is a little fuzzy; there are various versions, but the common thread in all is, prior to leaving Britain, an HBC officer named Aemilius Simpson was attending a dinner party that included fresh fruits. Liking the apple and grapes he'd eaten, Simpson saved seeds from both and, when he arrived at Fort Vancouver in late 1826, gave them to McLoughlin.[4] They were planted in early 1827. The grapes were, by 1832, growing immediately in front of the manager's residence, where they could climb the porch columns.[5]

Two key points: 1) these were table grapes, not wine grapes; table grapes, compared to wine grapes, are larger, less sweet, less acidic, have fewer seeds and a higher pulp/juice ratio, and 2) these grapevines and apple trees were started from seed, not cuttings. This is important, because grapes and apples—as well as most cultivated fruits—do not breed true. Planting seeds from a Golden Delicious or a Cabernet Sauvignon will not get you a tree or vine that bears those; propagation from cuttings is the only method.

Chief Factor's residence at Fort Vancouver. Restored to match an 1860 photograph, except that in 1860 there were considerably more grapevines. *National Park Service.*

Sure enough, the apples from these first-planted trees were reported to be sour by all who sampled them. The company did manage to acquire some better apple trees, probably by purchasing young potted trees from Spanish colonies farther south. (This is how three young peach trees were acquired in 1829.)[6]

The grapevines, despite their heterozygous origin, bore tasty fruit. Additional vines were planted at the north end of the garden outside the stockade. In 1836, Narcissa Whitman visited Fort Vancouver and reported, "At the opposite end of the garden is a good summer house covered with grapevines."[7] Contemporary maps of the grounds show the "summer house" to be a small structure, probably what we today would call a gazebo.

So, there weren't a lot of grapes growing at the fort during this period—not enough to make any quantity of wine, and not of the sort that you'd normally choose to use for wine. Anyone wishing to make wine might just as likely have used wild blackberries, elderberries or wintergreen. (*Gaultheria myrsinites*, which one historian claims—but without any source citation—"in early days made an excellent wine for the resident Hudson Bay Company employees.")[8]

Commencing in 1829, settlers began migrating into the Willamette Valley. Most of the first were former Hudson's Bay Company employees. A large percentage were French Canadians, a fact that inspired **Myth Number Two**: "The first winemakers in the Willamette Valley were French Canadians, former HBC fur-trappers who used cuttings from Fort Vancouver to plant vines and make wine." Again, the author has found no contemporary accounts of winemaking by these early settlers. Undoubtedly, many planted vine cuttings from the fort, but most of the fruit was probably consumed fresh or used in jelly rather than made into wine.

In 1836, Ewing Young began his distilling operation, and associated with this is **Myth Number Three**: "Ewing Young and partner Lawrence Carmichael were distilling brandy from wine." This one traces back to the 1977 book *Winemakers of the Pacific Northwest* written by J. Elizabeth Purser. On pages 153–54 appears the passage, "…there is a record of Ewing Young and Lawrence Carmichael setting up a still in 1835 which claimed to convert any wine to good brandy." This author had thoroughly researched Young's distilling operation for *Distilled in Oregon* and had never encountered this report; in fact, all contemporary accounts state that Young was making whiskey and that his operation commenced in late 1836, not in 1835. Methodist missionary Joseph Frost, in his memoirs, describes Young's activities in a two-page rant that "he addressed himself vigorously to the work—soaked, and sprouted, and dried his grain."[9] Those familiar with whiskey production will recognize this as the malting process—germinating grain to create enzymes that convert starch to sugar.

Young could not have obtained sufficient wine for a commercial distilling enterprise. (His plan was to trade distilled spirits to the natives in exchange for furs.) It takes about six gallons of wine to make one of brandy, and as we've seen, there wasn't a lot of locally produced wine available (assuming there was any at all). Furthermore, any wine that was being made would have not been available to Young; John McLoughlin, who'd been told that Young was a horse thief (not true, as it turned out), had ordered HBC employees to do no business with him, a proscription the ex-employees in the lower valley were expected to follow as well. These last would not have sold wine to Young even if they could; opposition to his project was strong, and a letter urging him to cease the operation was signed by twenty-eight individuals, a number described as "nearly every person in the settlement."[10] (Eleven of the signatories had French surnames.)

What was the origin of this "report" of brandy making? The author contacted Purser and asked her about it. She recalled the passage but not its source and, having disposed of her research notes many years ago, couldn't check. A reasonable guess is that Young, hearing that a local winemaker was unhappy with his wild wintergreen wine, offered to turn it into something better by distilling it. Unfortunately for posterity, someone who heard about this wrote it down.

In 1844, the provisional legislature passed a prohibition law that banned the sale or import of "ardent" (distilled) spirits. This was replaced in late 1846 by a law titled "An act to regulate the manufacture and sale of wine and distilled spirituous liquors." Distillers were required to pay an annual fee of $300, and though there was no license required to make wine, the fee to sell it was the same as for distilled spirits ($200 per year to sell quantities of five gallons or more, $100 to sell quantities less than that). These were considerable amounts, and the law's passage suggests that the majority of the population was neither interested in drinking wine nor sympathetic to those who were. The law probably reflects a religious bias; most of the population was Protestant, while the (presumably wine-drinking) French Canadians were mostly Catholic. Fortunately, the law was replaced in 1854 by one that required a license for only the sale of distilled spirits.

Viticulture in Oregon received a boost in 1847 when Henderson Luelling arrived with 350 cuttings of fruit and nut trees, including grapevines. The grapes were Isabella and Catawba,[11] both *vinifera x labrusca* hybrids. Luelling started his own vineyard in addition to selling cuttings from his nursery. In 1859, his partner William Meek entered two wines in the California state fair, one being a *blanc de noir* Isabella and the other made from currants. The Isabella won a second-tier award; Meek's currant wine won nothing.[12]

Returning to the French Canadian settlers in the lower Willamette Valley, we find most of them clustered about fifteen miles upriver from Oregon City, in an area which became known as "French Prairie." There were a number of towns established; two on the river were Butteville and Champoeg. The name of the latter was probably derived from a native Kalapuyan phrase that meant "place of yampah" (a type of wild carrot). Champoeg was the seat of the Oregon provisional government from 1841 to 1848; after Oregon became a United States territory in 1848, the capital was moved to Oregon City. Another town founded in the area was St. Paul, site of the first Catholic church in Oregon (1836). In 1847, the original log structure was replaced by one built of brick. Still standing, it's the oldest brick building in Oregon.

Most of the one hundred–plus French farmers in the area were growing grain (chiefly wheat), but it's likely that some were also growing grapes—initially the Fort Vancouver variety but later the hybrids brought

The spiritual center of French Prairie is the Catholic church in St. Paul. Constructed in 1847, it's the oldest brick building in Oregon. *Photo by the author.*

		NATIVE WINES, ETC.		
Exhibitor.	Residence.	Article.	Grade of Prem'm.	Prem'm.
Austin, J. C.	Sacramento	Cider... .	1st	Dip.
Baker & Cutting	San Francisco	Champagne cider	special	Dip.
Haraszthy, A.	Sonoma	Exhibit of wines	1st	S C 30
Haraszthy, A.	Sonoma	White wine, 1 year old	1st	S C 15
Haraszthy, A.	Sonoma	Red wine, 1 year old	2d	S C 10
Haraszthy, A.	Sonoma	Red wine, Menise	special	Dip.
Haraszthy, A.	Sonoma	White wine, Tokay	special	Dip.
Haraszthy, A.	Sonoma	Brandy, 1 year old	special	Dip.
Cole, J. B.	Sacramento	Lager beer	1st	Dip.
Knauth, J.	Sacramento	White wine, 1 year old	2d	S C 10
Keller, F.	Sacramento	White wine	2d	Dip.
Kohler & Co	San Francisco	White wine, 2 years old	special	S C 15
Meek, W.	Oregon	White Isabella, 1 year old	2d	Dipl'a
Sainsevaine Bros	Los Angeles	White wine, 2 years old	2d	10
Sainsevaine Bros	Los Angeles	White wine, sparkling... ..	1st	$15
Smith, A. P.	Sacramento	White wine	special	Dip.
Staunton, A.	Oregon	Red currant wine	special	Dip.
Smith & Co.	Sacramento	Jug ale	special	Dip.
Smith & Co.	Sacramento	Brown stout	special	Dip.
Thompson, S.	Napa	Currant wine	special	Dip.
Thompson, Wm. P.	Marysville	Red wine	special	Dip.
Vallejo, M. G.	Sonoma	Wine red, 1st class	2d	S C 15
Vallejo, M. G.	Sonoma	Wine white, 3 years old	1st	S C 15
Vallejo, M. G.	Sonoma	Wine white, 2 years old	1st	S C 15
Vallejo, M. G.	Sonoma	Wine red, 2 years old	1st	S C 15
Wilson, B. D.	Los Angeles	Wine white, 3 years old	2d	S C 10
Wilson, B. D.	Los Angeles	Wine red, 2 years old	2d	S C 10

The first time an Oregon wine won anything was at the California State Fair in 1859, when William Meek's blanc de noir Isabella took a second-place prize. *Public domain.*

in by Luelling. Whether they were making wine from these is debatable; although they were culturally predisposed to prefer wine to beer or hard apple cider, the grapes available to them would never produce anything more than *vin ordinaire*. That may have been sufficient for some of them, but surely many wished for something better.

What they needed was someone who would bring in better varieties of *vinifera*. Someone with some genuine wine expertise. Someone who could make better wine.

In 1853, they got their wish.

3

THE FRENCHMAN

J ean Jacques Mathiot was born in 1804 at his family's farm in Autechaux in eastern France. The farm was about sixty miles east of Dijon, the city at the northern end of the Burgundy winegrowing district. Autechaux is in the Franche-Comté region, an area where the primary red grapes are Pinot noir and Poulsard; today, the ratio of the former to the latter is about 10:1, but in Jean's time the percentage of Poulsard was probably higher than it is today. Chardonnay is the primary white grape. The climate is generally cooler and wetter than Burgundy, but the region is highly varied and there are warmer microclimates that mimic growing conditions in Burgundy. Grapevines are usually planted on south-facing slopes.[13]

The Mathiot family history does not record whether Jean's family was growing grapes or making wine, but even if they weren't it's certain that some of their neighbors were. Whatever exposure he had to viticulture must have kindled an interest, given his choice of vocations later in life.

In 1827, Jean married Catherine Vergon and went to live at her family's farm. Catherine was an only child and her father was nearly blind, so the burden of working the farm fell on Jean. His father-in-law died not long after the marriage, and Catherine inherited the thirty-acre property.

Jean and Catherine had four children over the next eleven years: a daughter, Eugénie, in 1828, and three sons, Adolphe (1833), Edouard (1837) and Pierre (1839).

In 1837, Jean decided to get into the wine trade and formed a partnership with his two brothers, Jacques and Pierre. They had a new building constructed to house the business, and according to Jean's son Pierre, "My father went about the country with a six-horse team to purchase wine while my uncle Pierre kept the books."[14]

The business was in trouble from the start. The new building's cost was over budget, and Jacques and Pierre made a habit of raiding the company funds. By mid-1838, the company was insolvent, and the brothers dissolved the partnership and sold the building.

Jean decided the family needed a fresh start, somewhere outside of France. In 1838, he visited Algeria (French territory since 1830) and, deciding against that, went to the United States in 1839. It was here that he chose to immigrate, and he returned to France to sell the farm and collect his family. They arrived in 1842 and settled in Ohio, where he acquired a 175-acre farm. The farm already had 100 acres under cultivation, to which Jean added a vineyard. Two more daughters were born to Jean and Catherine during the years in Ohio: Cephalie (1844) and Aline (1847).

The Mathiot farm was a prosperous enterprise—except for the grapes. Son Pierre writes:

> *He had the best appointed farm for miles around and about all heart could wish, but he had set out a vineyard and they did not do well. They would at times freeze to the ground. My Father could never be made to believe that a country was fit to live in unless he could raise grapes and small fruits and make wine.*
>
> *So he began to read books of travels, especially about Oregon, and the more he learned about the Country, the more he took it to be the promised land.*

In 1852, Jean sold the farm, packed up the family and left Ohio, taking a series of steamships to reach Nicaragua, traversing said country, and then two more steamships to reach Oregon. They arrived in Butteville in early 1853.

Why did Jean Mathiot choose Oregon instead of, say, northern California? Probably because the climate of the Willamette Valley was similar to his native Franche-Comté, a little cooler and wetter than Burgundy. Mathiot wanted a climate with which he was familiar so that he could raise grapes with which he was familiar.

In 1854, he acquired 132 acres on the south side of the river. (This section of the Willamette runs from west to east.) The chief feature of the

SAN JOSE
NURSERY.
FRUIT TREES.
ORNAMENTAL TREES.
ORNAMENTAL SHRUBS.
18,000 **ROSES.**

....ALSO....

GREENHOUSE PLANTS,
GRAPE-VINES,
ETC., ETC., ETC.

FOR SALE in lots to suit purchasers. TRADE
supplied at a liberal discount.

☞ I have the larest variety of Fruit and Ornamental
Trees, Shrubs, Roses, etc., that can be found in any one
Nursery in California.

Being determined to sell, my prices shall be very low
so as to give full satisfaction to my old customers as wel
as to new patrons.

₊ All Orders will be promptly attended to, and the
Trees well packed up in bundles or boxes—according to
size, and the distance they have to go—and delivered
free on board the steamer at Alviso. My Collection of

ROSES

received the FIRST PREMIUM at the State Fair held at
San Jose.

My Catalogue, giving a description of each variety I
have to sell, and giving information about transplanting
the prices, etc., can be had at the Nursery. Direct to
L. PREVOST,
San José, Cal.

*The prices in the catalogue are for trees of large size, for
smaller ones the price will be greatly reduced, and a still
further reduction made when taken by the quantity.

Agents.

MR. DELARIGNE, 64 Clay street, San Francisco.
C. W. LECOUNT, 99 Davis street, San Francisco.
MR. JACQUIER, Sonora. MR. A. VIENRICH, Oroville
The above named will have Trees to sell and will receive
and forward orders to me. [24

Louis Prevost was one of several
San Jose nursery owners offering
European grapevines during the late
1850s. *Public domain.*

property is "La Butte," a hill just west of Butteville with a peak elevation just over 400 feet above sea level. Jean planned to establish a vineyard on the south-facing side, but the hill was covered with forest, and clearing it took nearly four years (building a house and raising crops took time too). By early 1858, he was ready to start planting vines and took a steamship to San Francisco to buy some. He returned with $600 worth of cuttings ($17,259 in 2018 dollars). Evidently this was not enough to fill the vineyard, because son Adolphe made the same trip in 1859 and spent an additional $800 ($23,012).[15]

From whom did the Mathiots purchase their vines? By the end of the 1850s, there were vineyards and wineries scattered all around the San Francisco Bay area, along with nurseries that sold grapevine cuttings. The greatest concentration of these was around San Jose, and a number were owned by Frenchmen. Pierre Pellier, Louis Prevost and Antoine Delmas offered European vines in their nurseries; in 1858, Delmas's nursery had some 40,000 vines in 105 varieties.[16] Also in the area was the vineyard of Etienne Theé, begun in 1852 with Mission grapes, but supplemented in 1857–58 with vines acquired by Theé's son-in-law Charles Lefranc.[17] Lefranc is said to have acquired some of his vines in Champagne;[18] presumably these included Pinot noir, Pinot Meunier and Chardonnay, given the ubiquity of those varieties in Champagne. In addition to the properties owned by French immigrants, there were several others near San Jose, including one owned by the German immigrant Frank Stock, who had Riesling, Sylvaner and Traminer.

A little research would have informed Jean Mathiot that a trip down to San Jose would give him the best selection for the least amount of travel time and expense, and it's likely he did. Being able to converse with some of the nurserymen in his native tongue would have been an added bonus.

There's no record of what varieties were purchased. His first choice would have been grapes with which he was familiar (Pinot noir, Poulsard and Chardonnay), but these were not yet available in California in 1859. Beyond those, he would have favored anything cool climate compatible. Of the fifty varieties he is reported to have had in his vineyard,[19] likely candidates are Chasselas (white, pink and violet variants), Black Muscat, Red Traminer (Gewürztraminer is believed to be a mutation of this) and Riesling. What the other forty-plus varieties were is anyone's guess, and if it's true that Jean Mathiot was growing fifty varieties of grape, it suggests that he was trying a wide variety to see how they would do in the Willamette.

One variety of which we can be certain is Pinot Meunier (the basis for this certainty is divulged in a later chapter), a fact which increases the probability that he visited the Delmas nursery, because Delmas offered Pinot Meunier.[20] Among the vines purchased in 1858 and '59 were some originating from the cuttings taken from the anonymous vine we met in chapter 1.

Viticulturalist Adam Shipley visited the Mathiot vineyard in September 1869 and provided the following description:

> *The best vineyard in Oregon is situated near the Willamette river, at Butteville. It occupies the southeast slope of a high butte or hill, which rises out of the prairie. The vines, comprising about fifty kinds, all foreign, are planted about three feet apart each way, and are cultivated entirely by hand, and are trained to stakes. The pruning is very simple. Two or three canes are allowed to grow this season, and at the pruning season one of them is cut back to six or eight buds for fruiting next year; one of the others, with the cane which bore this year, is cut entirely away, and the remaining cane is cut to two or three buds, to grow two or three canes next year. The bearing canes are not tied up, but are allowed to lie on the ground with their load of fruit, and in consequence some of the grapes were damaged by our early rains. I visited this vineyard in September, and at that time the whole face of the hill was literally covered with the beautiful clusters, some of them weighing four pounds, and of all colors. It was a beautiful sight, and interested me exceedingly.*[21]

The Mathiots' vines would have started bearing around 1861, and presumably that's when wine production began. The customer base would have been mostly the French-speaking population of the area, and the wine was probably sold by the barrel to local farmers; some might have been

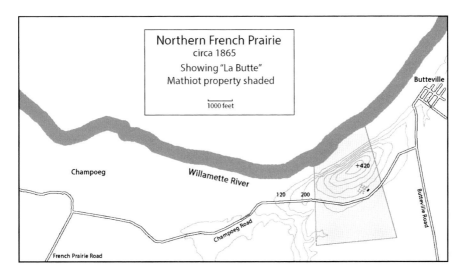

Location of Mathiot property. In 1861, half of Butteville and all of Champoeg were destroyed by flood. *Map by the author.*

sold to stores or taverns in St. Paul. (The two towns closest to the Mathiot farm—Champoeg and Butteville—had been destroyed by flood in 1861).

Sometime in the 1860s, the Mathiots acquired a still and began turning some of their wine into brandy. IRS tax assessment lists from 1867 show Edward (Edouard) Mathiot paying excise tax on grape brandy, and this is the first documented instance of anyone producing such in Oregon. The excise tax on grape brandy jumped from $0.50 per gallon to $2.00 in July 1866, a rate too high to turn a profit. It dropped back to $0.50 in July 1868, but by this time Edward Mathiot was evidently in the habit of underreporting production and thereby underpaying tax. On February 23, 1870, the IRS seized the still, along with 212 gallons of brandy and 900 gallons of wine. Edward was convicted, paid a $2,000 fine and spent a year in jail.[22]

A year after his incarceration ended, Edward married Julia Labbe. Hers was another of the French families of the area and was closely allied with the Mathiots. (One of Julia's brothers married one of Edward's sisters.)

Jean Mathiot died in 1876, wife Catherine in 1878. Both are buried in the Champoeg cemetery.

The Mathiots' wine production declined over the course of the 1870s; the agricultural schedule from the 1880 Census records only four acres of producing vines and 464 gallons of wine produced. The entry for the Mathiot farm shows a diversified enterprise, with oats, wheat, potatoes and apples, as well as dairy cows, swine and sheep.[23]

There was probably a declining customer base for the Mathiots' wine; the area was becoming progressively Anglicized, and those locals who drank wine now had the option of buying imported wine. (The rail line from Portland had reached Salem by 1870.) The temperance movement was also eroding the population of wine drinkers.

Another possible reason for the reduction in the Mathiots' wine production was that Edward did not share his father's passion for winemaking, although his reported response to a "circular" (questionnaire) associated with the 1880 Census suggests that he still took some pride in his winemaking efforts. This circular originated with Dr. William McMurtrie, whose *Statistics of Grape Culture and Wine Production in the United States* accompanied the publication of the 1880 Census. Fifteen thousand copies of the circular were distributed; a little less than half were returned.[24] McMurtrie had enlisted the assistance of local postmasters to distribute these, and it's certain that Edward Mathiot received one, given that older brother Adolphe was the postmaster for that part of Marion County. In his response, Edward is reported to have described Butteville as "the wine capital of Oregon."[25] Given that the agricultural schedule for 1880 shows no other winemakers in the area, it would seem that Edward felt his own efforts were sufficient to confer this honor on northwestern Marion County. The few published accounts of this claim fail to attribute it to Mathiot, and the wording implies this was an official assessment. These accounts originate **MYTH NUMBER FOUR**: "An 1880 farm report described the community of Butteville as the wine capital of Oregon." Anyone with knowledge of the 1880 statistics knew that Marion County's wine production of five hundred gallons was dwarfed by Jackson County's fifteen thousand gallons. If any community in Oregon deserved the title of "wine capital," it would be Jacksonville.[26]

Marion County within Oregon's Second Agricultural District, and in 1893 district commissioner R.D. Allen reported that the Mathiot vineyard was "about ten acres" and planted chiefly with Chasselas, Chasselas rose and Black Muscat.[27]

There are no written records of viticulture or winemaking by the Mathiots after 1893, though oral history holds that the vineyard was maintained until the 1930s.[28] Edward Mathiot died in 1912, but son Peter apparently continued growing grapes despite the advent of statewide prohibition in 1916; these were probably sold to those making wine at home. Peter died in 1931, and the farm was sold shortly thereafter.

Grave of Jean Mathiot, Champoeg cemetery. *Photo by the author.*

Jean Mathiot is an obscure figure in the history of Oregon winemaking. His was the Old World business model: a small-production rural winemaker, producing for a local customer base. This worked well enough in France, but Oregon in the latter half of the nineteenth century was a different place, with shifting demographics and advancing transportation technology. Nevertheless, he was a pioneer in choosing Oregon as the place where he would make his wine, believing it to have the right climate for the grapes he wanted to grow. It would be another hundred years before anyone else did the same.

4

FALSE DAWN

Peter Britt was born in Obstalden, Switzerland, in 1819. His was a farming family, but Peter had artistic inclinations and became a portrait artist. He was evidently not successful at this, because he joined the rest of his family when they immigrated to the United States in 1845. They settled Highland, Illinois, a mostly Swiss community that produced, among other things, wine from Catawba grapes.[29]

Peter Britt recognized the new technology of photography was going to replace portrait painting and studied the subject with professional photographer John Fitzgibbon. In 1852, Britt decided to go to Oregon, sharing a wagon with three other Swiss émigrés. When they reached eastern Oregon, two of the party declared they were unwilling to haul Britt's three hundred pounds of photo equipment any farther. The fourth member of the party was John Hug, a wagon master who converted the wagon into two carts, one for Britt and himself and one for the other two men. Upon reaching the Willamette, Britt and Hug turned south. Hug settled in Butteville, working first as a wagon master but eventually acquiring a farm and wife. Among other things, he grew apples and converted some of these into brandy; the 1867 tax assessment that lists Edward Mathiot has Hug on the same page.

Britt continued south, his destination being Jacksonville. Gold had been discovered in Jackson County that year, and he correctly guessed that the first thing a miner did after a successful strike was to buy a new suit, with the second thing being photographed wearing it.

Peter Britt (*at left*) entertaining friends in his garden. *SOHS #8267, courtesy of Southern Oregon Historical Society.*

Arriving in Jacksonville in November 1852 and recognizing the area's isolation, he acquired a mule team and began transporting goods from the coastal town of Crescent City, California. This was a lucrative enterprise, and after four years he sold his mules and was able to focus on his photography.[30] In 1859, he built a large house to replace his log cabin and, in 1861, sent money to his Swiss sweetheart, Amalia Grob, so that she could come to Oregon. They married upon her arrival, and when their first child was born the following year, Britt commemorated the event by planting a sequoia tree in his yard. The tree still exists and, at 205 feet in height, is the tallest sequoia in Oregon.[31]

Sequoia trees aren't the only thing Britt planted. Sometime in the late 1850s, he planted Mission grapes on his property in Jacksonville and, within a few years, began making wine. He was making more than his own family could drink and sold his surplus to friends and neighbors. Britt's home winemaking was the basis for **Myth Number Five**: "Oregon's first commercial winery was Valley View, founded by Peter Britt in the 1850s." Britt did start a commercial winery by that name, but it wasn't until 1873, well after the Mathiots started commercial production.

What prompted the founding of Valley View was a letter Britt received from the IRS that informed him of his "liability to pay a retail and wholesale License for selling wine of your own making."[32] Rather than give up winemaking, Britt decided to expand a vineyard he'd established on property purchased in 1871. The property, about 110 acres, was about a mile north of Jacksonville,[33] where there was a large hill with a southeast-facing slope. There were no more than 5 acres planted in vines, but by 1880 this had expanded to 15. During the mid-1880s, Britt added more *vinifera* varieties, including Cabernet Sauvignon, Malbec, Semillon, Sauvignon blanc, Zinfandel, Charbono, Mourvèdre, Petite Sirah, Riesling and Franc Pinot.[34] (This last was a generally accepted paranym for Pinot noir). By 1891, he'd added Cabernet Franc, Merlot and Traminer.[35] He continued to make the wine in his cellar; it's unclear whether he ever increased its storage capacity beyond three thousand gallons.

Britt was the quintessential nineteenth-century entrepreneur. He promoted his wines, bottled them and sold them not just in Oregon but neighboring states as well. He picked up a contract to supply sacramental wine to the Catholic churches in Oregon. In short, he did all the things that Jean Mathiot did not do and is thus a prominent figure in the history of Oregon winemaking.

The agricultural schedule from the 1880 Census shows that Britt was not the only winemaker in the Rogue Valley. Kentuckian James Miller had the largest vineyard, at twenty acres, and produced 2,500 gallons of wine in 1879 and sold 600 pounds of grapes. His neighbor Raphael Morat, from southwest France, also produced 2,500 gallons of wine, but most of this was destined to become brandy. Grandville Sears sold 5 tons of grapes and made 250 gallons of wine, and William Leever sold 5,000 pounds of grapes and

Harvest in the Britt vineyard, circa 1880. *SOHS #4534, courtesy of Southern Oregon Historical Society.*

made 40 gallons. John Cordwell is recorded as making 150 gallons of wine despite not owning a vineyard. There were plenty of sources for Cordwell's grapes; the schedule records thirteen additional vineyards each producing from 100 to 2,000 pounds of grapes.[36]

Clearly Jacksonville was the "wine capital of Oregon," but why? Two reasons: first, the Rogue Valley remained isolated until the mid-1880s, because work on the rail line from Portland ceased with the stock market crash of 1872. The line had reached Roseburg that year but had not yet crested Grant's Pass. Transport into the valley was via wagon or mule, an expensive option that gave a competitive advantage to locally produced goods. *Distilled in Oregon* describes how this encouraged the local distilling industry; the same advantage was enjoyed by the local vintners.

The second reason was the Rogue Valley's climate being similar to northern California—a little cooler and wetter, but close enough that varieties that grew well in northern California could be planted in the Rogue Valley with a reasonable expectation of success.

In 1890, the Southern Oregon State Board of Agriculture published "The Resources of Southern Oregon." This report provided some additional information about viticulture in the area. Miller and Morat had

Unidentified vineyardist (possibly Raphael Morat) in Jackson County, late 1800s. *SOHS #12777, courtesy of Southern Oregon Historical Society.*

a new neighbor growing grapes and making wine, this being Emile Barbe. According to the report, Miller and Barbe sold their wine for thirty cents to one dollar per gallon. Morat converted most of his wine into brandy, which he sold for two to five dollars per gallon "according to age." The report claims that Miller grew about twenty varieties of grapes, but the only two mentioned are "Sweetwater" (Chasselas) and "Miller Mission," a hybrid Miller created by crossing Mission with some unidentified grape.[37]

Many of the growers were selling their grapes locally, but with the railroad having reached the area in 1885, they were also shipping to Portland as well.

The viticultural portion of the report concludes with the optimistic forecast:

> *With the hills of Jackson, Josephine and Douglas* [Counties] *dotted with vineyards and beautiful villas, and the valleys rich in harvests of wonderous fruitage, the castled Rhine will need to look to her laurels in the realm of song, while the classical vales of Italy and the sunny slopes of France will find a rival in the land of the fabled West.*[38]

Fourteen years later, the *Oregonian* was no less enthusiastic:

> *Southern Oregon, particularly the Rogue River Valley, is in parts so like the Cote D'Or portion of Burgundy, where the best wine is made, that a Burgundian has never passed that way without saying, "Ma belle France." Some day a Burgundy wine will be made there in sufficient quantities to warrant a wide sale.*[39]

An accurate prediction, but it's doubtful the writer ever expected it would be ninety years before it came true.

Viticulture continued to flourish in the Rogue Valley, with 428 tons of grapes produced in 1899, but wine production was declining, with only 5,990 gallons produced that year,[40] about a third of the amount produced in 1880. (This may be an apples-to-oranges comparison; see the discussion at the end of this chapter.) Prohibition was gathering momentum, and the customer base for wine was diminishing. Another factor was the deaths of the area's most prolific winemakers; Morat and Barbe died in 1898, Miller in 1900 and Britt in 1905. Emil Britt was not interested in continuing with the winery and closed it in 1906.

Latecomers to the area were two additional Frenchmen, Joseph Ginet and August Petard. Ginet founded Plaisance Orchard in 1898, spent several years clearing an area for a vineyard, went to France in 1904 and returned with vine cuttings from his native Savoie.[41]

August Petard originally came to the area to prospect for gold, but he eventually bought land and planted a vineyard. He sold most of his grapes to Portland buyers but made a small amount of wine for his own use.[42]

Mention should also be made of Medford amateur winemaker John Demmer, a real estate salesman whose Riesling won a silver medal at the Lewis and Clark Exposition in 1905.[43]

Moving north into Douglas County, the first viticulturalist of record was Jesse Applegate. A prominent early Oregonian, he was a member of the provisional legislature and is best known for blazing the Applegate Trail, a safer alternative route for the last leg of the Oregon Trail. Applegate and his wife settled in northern part of the Umpqua Valley in 1849 and began raising livestock. A severe freeze in 1874 killed most of his stock, and he sold the property, moving to a forty-acre tract high on the side of Mount Yoncalla.[44] The Applegates built a cabin and engaged in small-scale farming. In 1876, nephew George Applegate brought 1,200 grapevines from California, and Jesse started a vineyard with these.[45] The first crop of grapes was destroyed by insects, and it may be the case that Applegate, already in his sixties, did not persist with the effort. There are no subsequent accounts of his viticultural efforts. He died in 1888.

The most prominent Umpqua Valley winemakers were three Germans, Adam Doerner and Edward and John von Pessl. Edward von Pessl (born 1862) arrived first, in 1883, with brother John (1864) immigrating the following year. They worked for several Napa Valley wineries, then sometime

Variously identified as the Petard or Ginet vineyard, circa 1900, Jackson County. *OWHA collection, donation of Joe and Suzi Ginet.*

in the mid-1880s moved up to Douglas County and started their own winery near Cleveland, a town about eight miles northwest of Roseburg. They planted vines brought from California; these reportedly included Zinfandel, Riesling and "Sauvignon" (probably Sauvignon blanc or Sauvignon vert).[46] It appears they never completely cut ties to California; Edward von Pessl is still on the Napa County voter roll as late as 1892.

Sometime in 1888, they were visited by Adam Doerner, who'd immigrated the previous year, disembarking in Philadelphia on December 12.[47] Inspired by the von Pessls' success, Doerner purchased property near Melrose (two miles south of Cleveland) and began the process of starting a winery. He spent the next several years shuttling between Melrose and the Napa wineries where he was employed, bringing vines with him when returning to Oregon. (The completion of the Oregon–California railroad in 1887 made this possible.) Although his operation remained small (the vineyard was reported to be only one acre), Doerner acquired a good reputation for his winemaking, using techniques such as destemming before crushing and fermenting only free-run juice. He also made his own barrels.[48] His was a small-scale operation, making wine for his family, friends and neighbors. Sunday afternoons, many would gather at the Doerner farm to drink wine and beer.

Sometime in the early 1890s, Doerner and the von Pessl brothers partnered to start a distillery. The Cleveland Distilling Company described itself as "manufacturers and dealers in pure brandies and whiskies"; presumably, they made the brandy from their own wine and bought whiskey from other producers.

In 1903, the von Pessl brothers decided to terminate their Oregon winemaking operation and sold their property. Edward returned to California; the 1910 Census finds him owning a farm near San Jose, producing fruit and hay. In 1920, he was back in Douglas County, apparently retired (occupation given as "none"). He died there in 1929. Brother John moved to Missouri; the 1910 Census lists his occupation as "wine grower." By 1920, he had moved to Colorado and was running a dairy farm. He died in 1934.

Adam Doerner continued making wine right up until the imposition of statewide prohibition in 1916.

Returning to the Willamette Valley, we see a different pattern of viticulture. Despite demonstrated success with *Vitis vinifera*, most growers favored native American or hybrid varieties, believing *vinifera* would not ripen. Some of them grew *vinifera*, but it was a minority percentage of their vines.

Cleveland Distilling Co.

Manufacturers of and Dealers in

PURE BRANDIES AND WHISKIES

LIQUORS FOR FAMILY AND MEDICINAL PURPOSES

A SPECIALTY.

ALL FIRST CLASS DRUG STORES AND SALOONS HANDLE OUR GOODS.

Goods delivered in quantities of one gallon or more. Orders from Town and Country Solicited, and will be promptly attended to.

Office and Salesroom, NORTH ROSEBURG.

VON PESSL & DOERNER, Proprs.

During the 1890s Adam Doerner and the von Pessl brothers operated a distillery, using their own wine to make brandy. *Public domain.*

Sunday afternoon at the Doerner residence, circa 1895. Adam Doerner is seated at left, with young son Adolph to his right. Directly behind Adam Doerner is John von Pessl, with Edward von Pessl to his left. *OWHA collection, donation of Shelley and Mike Wetherell.*

The most prominent Willamette viticulturalist was Adam Shipley. Born in Pennsylvania in 1826 and raised in Ohio, Shipley arrived in Portland in the early 1850s. By 1854, he had a job (postmaster) and a wife, Celinda Hines. In 1862, they acquired 130 acres east of Oswego and started a farm. The property included a hill (today known as Cook's Butte), and Shipley realized its south-facing slope would be a good spot for a vineyard.

From the outset, Adam Shipley favored native American and hybrid varieties, but he did experiment with *Vitis vinifera*. (He bought cuttings from the Mathiots and spent time in their wine cellar,[49] perhaps to educate himself on winemaking). It's reported that he planted over forty varieties in his own vineyard.[50]

Shipley was a prolific writer, and his target audience was not winemakers but the typical diversified farmer. There was a big market for table and jelly grapes, and for these purposes Shipley recommended native types such as Concord or Delaware and hybrids such as Isabella.[51] The Concord, with its resistance to disease and pests and its high yields, was his top recommended grape.[52]

Not that he didn't have advice for those wanting to grow *Vitis vinifera* wine grapes. Black Muscat (usually called "Black Hamburg" in that time and place) was his recommended dark grape, with his recommended white being Chasselas blanc (unfortunately often called "Royal Muscadine" a confusing practice, given that "muscadine" is a name commonly used for the species *Vitis rotundifolia*). Though warning that both varieties were prone to mildew, Shipley believed that with careful site selection, well-drained soil and proper cultivation, local growers could produce first-class grapes. "France herself cannot produce finer Muscadines and Hamburgs than grow on the sunny hills of Western Oregon."[53]

In 1888, Shipley was appointed to the board of regents at the State Agricultural College in Corvallis (the college later became Oregon State University), leaving his son in charge of the farm. Adam Shipley died in 1894 at age sixty-seven. His son sold the farm to James and Susan Cook in 1900. The Cooks used some of the acreage to raise cattle and swine but continued to cultivate Concord grapes on the property. Over the course of the twentieth century, most of the farm was sold off for residential development (the southeast side of Cook's Butte is now covered with expensive homes), but the original house and barn of 1862 have been preserved and are surrounded by a vineyard. The grape is Maréchal Foch, a *riparia x rupestris x vinifera* hybrid; Adam Shipley would probably approve.

In 1872, the Salem newspaper *Willamette Farmer* reported on some grapes submitted by Albany grower John Millard. These included the American and hybrid varieties Concord, Iona, Israella, Diana, Adirondack, Rebecca, Delaware and Allen's Hybrid, and the European varieties Black Hamburg (Black Muscat), Chasselas, Riesling, Red Riesling, Black St. Peter (Zinfandel) and Miller's Burgundy. This last is described as having "a cotton down on both sides of its leaves; hence the name Miller's grape." This is, of course, Pinot Meunier, and it's likely Millard obtained his vines from the Mathiots.

The *Willamette Farmer* article concludes:

> *It was long thought Oregon could not grow the foreign grape. This opinion, experience has proven to be incorrect. Oregon, in our humble opinion, will,*

ere long, be a noted grape-growing country; and especially, we think, as a wine growing country. Our equable climate, our dry, high hills, must produce, when fairly tried, the very finest wine vineyards.[54]

Lane County grower D.W. Coolidge writes in 1901:

Sixteen years ago, when I moved out into the hills south of Eugene, and told some of my farmer friends that I was going to devote one of the choicest spots of my limited area to a vineyard, they tried to dissuade me, at the same time informing me that they had tried grape-growing, and that on account of the cool summers, grapes would never get sweet and only in exceptional seasons could any grapes fit for table use be raised.

My first step, after preparing a warm sunny spot on the southeast side of a hill, was to procure from a vineyardist in Napa valley, California, plants of his best early grapes of the Vinifera *or foreign type, and at the same time secure from an extensive grape grower of western New York plants of his best American varieties. When the vines were three years old not one of my neighbors was so astonished at the large beautiful clusters of delicious grapes—red, white and blue—as myself, and when put on the Eugene market nine out of ten purchasers supposed they were getting California fruit.*[55]

Coolidge grew mostly American varieties, but goes on to say, "My favorites of all grapes grown in the Willamette valley are two foreign varieties, the Chasselas Neuschatel, a white or green grape of the sweetwater type; but much superior to it in both size of fruit and flavor is the Black Malvoiseie [Cinsault]." Coolidge was not a winemaker, but perhaps some of his customers were using his *vinifera* grapes to make their own wine.

In his 1893 account, Commissioner Allen reports on several other Second Agricultural District vineyards besides that of the Mathiot family. The only other to grow *vinifera* grapes was one situated on the south slope of Lone Butte near Mount Angel, below the Benedictine abbey founded in 1884. Local farmer Jacob Cornelius, one of many recent German immigrants to the area, was growing "several varieties of foreign grapes," including Black Hamburg.[56]

Missing from Allen's report is the vineyard of August Aufranc, a Swiss immigrant who arrived with his family in 1884. Located just east of Salem, the vineyard included Chasselas, Red Burgundy and Concord.[57] (The "Red

Burgundy" was probably Pinot noir.) Aufranc was both a wine and brandy maker, but he made his brandy from apples, pears and prunes.[58]

More typical are the vineyards of Daniel Loveridge of Eugene and Milton Fitzgerell of Silverton, who were growing native varieties for use as table grapes.[59]

Farther north, in the lower Willamette Valley, growers John Broetje and Wilbur Newell, in their respective sections in the 1901 publication "The Grape in Oregon," advise against planting *vinifera* in the area, citing problems with mildew and ripening.[60]

Others believed that the issue was unresolved. D.H. Stearns, editor of the periodical *Fruits and Flowers of Oregon and Washington*, wrote in 1892, "Of late, some Germans have commenced grape culture on the foothills, not far from Forest Grove, and their experience will go far to decide the question."[61]

The Germans to which Stearns was referring were Frederick Adolph Reuter and his son Ernest. Reuter arrived in Oregon in 1886, with the rest of his family joining him the following year.[62] The Reuters acquired a farm on the southern side of David Hill, a large formation northwest of Forest Grove, the peak of which is only fifteen feet shy of qualifying as a mountain. The hill is named after Frederick David, a German immigrant who planted grapes in the area during the late 1870s.[63] The author has found no reports of what sort of grapes were raised by David or whether he produced any wine.

The Reuters, on the other hand, were definitely making wine. Their vineyard was planted with the *vinifera* varieties Sweetwater (Chasselas), Zinfandel, Burgundy (Pinot noir), Black Hamburg (Black Muscat), Muscatel, Red Mountain (unknown), Chasselas Fountainbleu (a.k.a. Golden Chasselas or Chasselas de Thomery) and Muscat, as well as with the hybrid Delaware.[64]

The Reuters' wines won a few awards. At the 1901 Pan-American Exposition in Buffalo, New York, they received bronze medals for their Burgundy and Muscat[65] and received a silver medal in 1905 at the Lewis and Clark Exposition in Portland for a "collective exhibit of wine."[66]

But here's where it starts to get dodgy. An *Oregonian* reporter interviewed Adolph Reuter sometime during the week of October 24, 1904, and in the following Sunday edition appeared:

A. Reuter, who had been making and selling from his cellar pure and nourishing wine for 15 years, decided at the time of the Omaha Exposition [1898] that he would send a few dozen bottles of his wine along to help out the Oregon exhibit. There were so few of them that it was hardly thought worth while at first to place them in competition with the imposing rows of bottles from California, New York and other wine producing communities. But when the judges tested the modest little exhibition of Rhine wines from Oregon, they never hesitated, but said: "Here is a wine pure and delicate in quality, with a perfect color and a bouquet unrivaled." And they gave the wine first prize.[67]

Checking the Omaha fair's list of award-winning exhibitors reveals two interesting facts: first, the award, for "various sorts of wines" was not awarded to Reuter but to the State of Oregon (perhaps this is what Reuter meant by "helping out"). Second, the wine did not receive "first prize" but instead won a silver medal.

The story becomes even more interesting at this point, and here we confront **MYTH NUMBER SIX**: "Forest Grove winemakers Adolph and Ernest Reuter received a silver [some say gold] medal for their Riesling [some say Pinot blanc] at the 1904 St. Louis world's fair." This is the most infamous of all the myths, famous because of its wide dissemination (it appears in numerous books, websites and even on a panel display created by the Oregon Historical Society) and infamous because it originated as a lie.

Summary results for the judging at the Louisiana Purchase Exposition (a.k.a. St. Louis World's Fair) were released on or about Monday, October 24, 1904. (The *Oregonian* ran an article titled "Prizes for Oregon" on the twenty-fifth.) Later in the week, detailed results were released, and on the twenty-ninth newspapers began publishing these. The *Oregonian* had a short article on page five announcing that the Dodson-Braun company had won a grand prize for its pickles and on page ten had an article announcing that the Baldwin company of Hay Creek, Oregon, had won prizes for its sheep. Two days later, the *Sunday Oregonian* ran a long article, "Making of Wine in the Chehalem Hills of Oregon," which prominently features the Reuters' winery. Nowhere is there any mention of a prize being awarded in St. Louis. In fact, examination of every issue of the *Oregonian* during the two weeks following October 29 fails to find any article announcing the award of a medal to the Reuters.

The fair's list of award winners reveals why: no wines from Oregon won anything.[68] Why not? The catalogue of exhibitors shows no wines from Oregon were entered.[69]

What was the origin of this myth? Ernest Reuter was briefly interviewed in 1906 by a reporter from the *Oregon City Enterprise*, who wrote:

A.E. Reuter of Forest Grove arrived Monday morning. In Oregon City for a few days visit with friends. Mr. Reuter has the largest vineyard on David's Hill near Forest Grove. His wines are famous all over the country and have received a gold medal from the Paris Exposition of 1900, and also prizes of distinction and medals from the Chicago, Pan American, St. Louis, and the Lewis and Clark Exposition.[70]

Whether the Reuters won anything at the Paris fair is easy enough to check, because H.W. Wiley, a chemist with the U.S. Department of Agriculture, published a paper titled "American Wines at the Paris Exposition of 1900." Neither the list of winning wines nor the list of American wines entered shows a wine from the Reuters or any other Oregon winemaker.[71]

As for the Chicago fair (the Columbian Exposition of 1893), a check of the catalogue of exhibitors finds no Oregon wines there either.[72]

The Reuters were probably making decent wine; it just wasn't as famous as they claimed. Nevertheless, the winery was a popular destination for many residents of the Forest Grove area; they would pack a lunch on Sundays, go to the winery, buy some wine and then picnic among the vines.

The *Sunday Oregonian* article gives a description of the Reuters' winemaking methods:

The big baskets filled with dead-ripe grapes from the well-laden vines are sledded to the vault, where they are dumped into a hopper without a bottom, leaving the bunches rest on a wire netting with a mesh big enough so that when the hopper is drawn back and forth across it the berries will drop from the stem and fall-through into huge vats. The berries are opened by the rubbing, and all that is necessary is to pour more on top till the vat is full.

There they lie till they have "worked." To help this process along sometimes a highly flavored grape in which the germ of fermentation works readily is placed with the rest to set the fermentation going. And there the vats are left till the sediment is at the bottom and the moment that sign of the end of the quick fermentation is shown, the wine is drawn off into barrels and the slow fermentation begins.

The slow fermentation requires some watching, but it is not great. Each year the wine has to be drawn off into new and clean barrels, and it is better after three years to bottle it, for then it will age quicker.

To tell the plain truth, little of the wine is ever bottled. It is sold in kegs from the vineyards, trundled off and drunk.[73]

The press of that era typically extolled the superiority of local products over those from elsewhere, and the *Oregonian* was no exception, describing the Reuters' wine as "a wine with a bouquet California could never equal." The most successful wines are listed as Muscatel, Riesling, Zinfandel, Burgundy and Hamburg.

The article claims there were about a dozen "winegrowers" on David Hill, with almost as many to the south in the Chehalem Hills and another three to the northeast in Mountaindale. Twenty-five winemakers in the area seems like a lot, considering that the 1899 wine production for Washington County was only 4,490 gallons, 1,500 less than Jackson County. With Washington County's grape production being 969 tons, the highest in the state,[74] it's probable most of the growers were producing grapes for table, jelly and juice, not for wine. The 1900 Census agricultural schedules would tell us who was making wine and how much they were making, but these were destroyed in 1919 because of storage issues. (The agricultural schedules for that census were reported to weigh 100 tons.)[75]

Another *Oregonian* article, from 1908, "Viticulture in Willamette Valley," lists some of the growers in the Forest Grove area. In addition to Adolph Reuter, J.A. Peterson, A. Anderson, F. Biled, R. Holischer and William Koppel are reported to "have large and profitable vineyards."[76] The article describes viticulture in general and states that few grapes are grown for the purpose of making wine. It does mention that "[o]ne vineyardist who has given considerable attention to that industry made 110 barrels of wine this Fall from six acres of grapes, mostly Sweetwater [Chasselas]. He finds that it takes about 600 pounds of grapes to make a barrel of wine." Unhelpfully, the article does not give the name of the winemaker or the size of the barrel.

Besides the Reuters, the author has been able to identify only two additional Forest Grove–area winemakers. The first is Frederick Stettler of Mountaindale, a Swiss immigrant who arrived in 1890. Stettler's winemaking received no press until the advent of Prohibition; we'll check back with him in chapter 6. The second is Jacob Jungen, another Swiss. According to family history, Jungen grew Chasselas and made about 360 gallons of wine per year.[77]

Moving east, up the Columbia River, we reach the Gorge, that narrow portion of the river's domain where it traverses the Cascades. At the east end of the Gorge is the city of The Dalles, where the three Sandoz brothers arrived from Switzerland in 1878. They started a farm several miles south of town, growing mostly vegetables and fruit.[78] They were also growing Zinfandel and making wine for themselves, friends and neighbors.[79]

Sometime in the late 1890s, another vineyard was started just north of the Sandoz property. The vineyard was on the property of Theodore Mesplie, a Frenchman (born 1830) who'd originally come to Oregon in the early 1850s to mine gold. His older brother Toussiant (1823) was the Catholic priest at The Dalles and encouraged Theodore to come to the area and take advantage of then available land grants. He arrived in 1852 and claimed the property that later contained the vineyard.[80]

The vineyard itself was the creation of Luigi "Louis" Comini, who was born in Lombardy in 1865 and immigrated to the United States in 1884. He settled in Wilmington, Delaware, where he met a local Italian woman, Caterina "Lena" Pino. They wed in 1889 and arrived in The Dalles sometime between the birth of their second child (August 1892, Wilmington) and their third (June 1894, Wasco County).[81] Luigi, a stonecutter, had come to the area to work on the locks being constructed on the river. Father Mesplie offered this new member of his congregation work making gravestones for the Catholic cemetery.

Sometime later, Theodore Mesplie hired Comini to put in his vineyard. Comini's qualifications are unknown; perhaps he was the only one willing to do it. We know the vineyard was planted with Zinfandel (probably from cuttings obtained from the Sandoz vineyard), but the caption for a 1911 photograph of the vineyard states that eighteen varieties were planted; what the other seventeen were is unknown. (There is reason to believe the grapes were exclusively Zinfandel.) Once the vines began bearing, Comini became the winemaker as well, supplying communion wine to the church. His primary occupation remained masonry; the 1910 Census lists him as owning his own business as well as a mortgage-free house.

Theodore Mesplie died in 1914 and daughter Celia inherited the vineyard. She allowed Luigi Comini to continue to manage the vineyard and make wine.

Moving farther upriver, the next place we find viticulture is the Walla Walla Valley, most of which lies north of the Oregon-Washington border. Grapevines were brought here in 1859 by Alvin Roberts, a native of Ohio (born 1832). Roberts arrived in the Portland area in 1853 and, like Luigi Comini, started a gravestone cutting business (a strange coincidence, that). In 1855, he enlisted in the army to serve in the Yakima War, a conflict between the U.S. government and an alliance of tribes in eastern Oregon and Washington. Much of the action took place in the Walla

Luigi Comini did well with his masonry business. Here he is at the wheel of his 1911 Buick, one of only two automobiles in Wasco County at the time. *Courtesy of the Comini family.*

Walla Valley, and Roberts must have felt the area had a good potential for agriculture. When the war ended in 1858, he returned to Portland where he married Martha Baxter in September, and in 1859 he went to French Prairie, where he purchased *Vitis vinifera* grapevines from "the French vineyardist at Champoig."[82] This would have been Jean Mathiot, because the Mathiots would have been the only source near Champoeg for any quantity of *vinifera*. (It may well be that Adolphe Mathiot's 1859 California vine-buying trip was both necessitated and financed by the sale of vines to Roberts.)

Roberts arrived in Walla Walla in 1859 with his wife and vines and established a farm and nursery. He ordered additional vines from France, as well as acquiring native and hybrid varieties, and eventually had some eighty varieties growing.[83] In 1871, he wrote:

> *The very choicest of European grapes ripen in the greatest perfection, without special care or protection, and are entirely free from mildew and every form of disease. The American grapes succeed equally well, but in comparison with the European grapes are very inferior fruit. But finer Concord, Delaware, Catawba, Isabella, and some twenty other varieties, were never seen than we produce here at Walla Walla.*[84]

In 1860, gold was discovered in a nearby part of Idaho (the Clearwater River basin), and the town of Walla Walla became a stopover for miners going to and from the goldfields. Many of the prospectors were European, and their taste for wine created something of a viticulture boom. By 1880, all twenty-six of the town's saloons offered locally produced wine.[85]

The majority of this wine was produced in Washington territory, but in the Oregon part of the Walla Walla Valley there were four grower-vintners recorded in the 1880 agricultural census. In the Cottonwood precinct of Umatilla County were two Germans: Matthias Albrecht, who produced 1,200 gallons of wine in 1879, and Jacob Zinc, who produced 150 gallons. In Milton, there was New Yorker William Cowl, who produced 1,200 gallons, along with German John Ostertag, who made 450.[86]

Alvin Roberts's belief that the vines needed no special care was sadly mistaken. In the winter of 1883–84, bitterly cold temperatures killed nearly all of the vines, and most of the survivors died the following winter. With the gold rush winding down and the bypassing of Walla Walla by the new rail line, there was little motivation to replant grapevines. The 1900 Census's agricultural report shows no wine produced in Umatilla County in 1899.

The peak period of Oregon's pre-Prohibition winemaking was from 1890 to 1904. During that period, there were over twenty individuals growing and making wine from *Vitis vinifera*. Most of them were immigrants, and most of the winemakers were in southern Oregon. They and their customers, probably mostly immigrants as well, wanted the kind of wine they'd been drinking in Europe and were willing to make the effort to grow the right grapes. They knew what they doing; they put their vineyards on well-drained south-facing slopes and planted early ripening varieties suited to the local climate. Some of them certainly made good wine; after all, in the three world fairs that the Reuters *actually entered*, they won silver medals at two and a bronze in the third.

Some Oregon wine was sold at outlets other than the wineries. The December 23, 1889 issue of the *Morning Oregonian* has an advertisement on page 5, column 2, for "Simon's best Oregon wine." The address given, 255 Morrison, was in downtown Portland; the price was $4.50 per case. The January 6, 1903 edition ran an article about Oregon products destined for an exhibit in Osaka, Japan; in the list appeared "Blumauer & Hoch, Oregon Wine."[87] Blumauer & Hoch was the largest wholesaler of liquor in Portland[88] and sold mostly Kentucky bourbon but other alcoholic beverages as well.

How much wine was being made in Oregon during this period is difficult to determine. The figure given in the 1900 Census agricultural report is 21,219 gallons for 1899, which is equivalent to the amount produced by two average-sized modern Oregon wineries. There are, however, some problems with this figure. First, it represents only "farm" production; commencing in 1900, output from "wineries" was recorded on the manufacturing schedules. The author has not been able to determine the difference between a "farm" and a "winery," but the definition of the latter was apparently fairly broad, because the report states that the amount made on farms is "only a small portion of that made in the country."[89] How many of Oregon's winemaking operations qualified as "wineries" is unknown. Only the information recorded on the agricultural and manufacturing schedules would provide the answers, and those were destroyed in 1919.

Second, much of the wine production was likely not reported. The was no excise tax on wine at the time, and no government agency made a great effort to track its production.

Despite these considerations, it's doubtful there was much more than thirty thousand gallons made for sale in 1899. This would be the output of only three average-sized modern Oregon wineries. (But then, the state's population in 1900 was only one-tenth of what it is today; on a per-capita basis, this would be equivalent to thirty modern wineries.)

It's tempting to speculate about what would have happened with the state's winemaking industry had it been allowed to continue unfettered. It might be that by concentrating on varieties that did better here than in California (Chasselas, Pinot noir and so forth), Oregon might well have found its niche in the winemaking world a century ago. As we've seen, there was no shortage of optimism about the state's future in the wine industry, but the sunny predictions being made were by those who'd failed to notice the dark clouds gathering on the horizon.

5

THE LIPS THAT TOUCH WINE…

The prohibition movement had its roots in the temperance movement of the late eighteenth and early nineteenth centuries. The temperance movement itself traces back to the writings of Benjamin Rush, a prominent American physician of the late eighteenth century who published in 1784 a slender book with the long title *An Enquiry into the Effects of Spiritous Liquors upon the Human Body, and Their Influence upon the Happiness of Society*. Rush was not opposed to all alcoholic beverages; he believed that beer, wine and hard cider were perfectly acceptable, even beneficial, when consumed in moderation and with meals. This was the original concept of "temperance," the dictionary definition of which includes the synonym "moderation." The early members of the movement shared this reasonable view (recall the Oregon prohibition law of 1844–47 applied to only distilled spirits), but beginning in the 1830s the goal of temperance activists began to shift to complete prohibition of all alcoholic beverages. This shift was probably inevitable; the psychology of zealotry is one of all-or-nothing-think and does not tolerate compromise.

This inflexibility probably did the movement more harm than good. This was an era during which the only safe beverages either contained alcohol or were made with near-boiling water (in essence, coffee and tea), and telling people they should drink only water or unfermented beverages was essentially the same as telling them to get sick and die. Such pronouncements were received with skepticism, and rightly so.

Not that there wasn't a problem with excessive alcohol use. Drunkenness was endemic in nineteenth-century America, and the effects on health and family were ruinous. The reasons for it were not a mystery; the livelihoods of most men of the era, whether on a farm or in a factory, were grueling, and most were tired and sore at the end of a ten-plus-hour day. Self-medicating with alcohol was how many coped, and this was facilitated by a profusion of saloons.

Many of the clergy, whose sedentary profession made them oblivious to such considerations, were quick to jump on the temperance bandwagon. Lyman Beecher, a preacher from New England, made a highly successful career of impugning the morality of those who drank. Again, this tactic often backfired; there are few quicker ways to alienate someone than to accuse them of immorality for drinking something that alleviated pain-induced insomnia.

Wine presented a particularly irksome conundrum to prohibitionists of the Bible-thumping variety. The Bible has a number of inconvenient passages that describe Jesus drinking wine, the most notable being those describing the Last Supper with his disciples, during which he equates the wine with his blood. These passages were frequently cited by the more rational Christians of the era, including a few clergymen. In Oregon, pastor Robert Stevens, in an article published in the August 19, 1881 issue of the *Albany State Rights Democrat*, argues that the total prohibition advocated by organizations such as the Woman's Christian Temperance Union was not only a violation of what was originally meant by "temperance" but also not Christian:

> *God has no where commanded men to abstain from wine, but He does command the temperate use of it. And every Christian by Christ's command is bound to partake of it at the Holy Communion, and to refuse to partake of the bread and wine is to violate His dying command. He makes no exception: "drink ye all of it."*[90]

Referencing the WCTU's intolerance of anyone adhering to the original concept of temperance, Stevens goes on to argue that this exclusionary policy is counterproductive:

> *[G]ood laws and moderate restrictions could easily be obtained, if the intolerance of the advocates of total abstinence did not prevent those who wish to aid temperance from joining their ranks. We would like to see the drunkard who beats his wife, whipped at the whipping post when he*

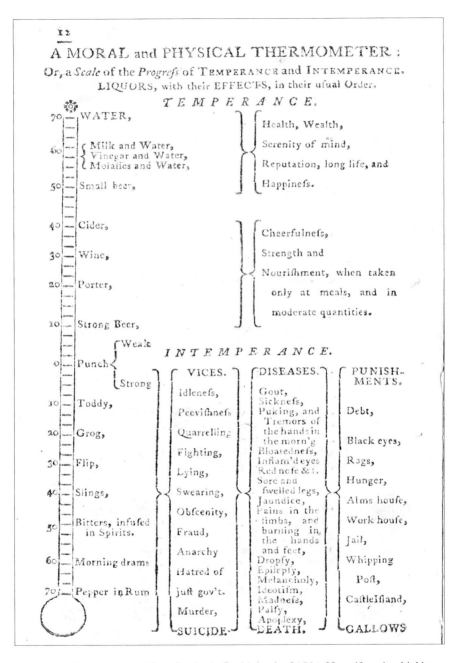

The "Moral Thermometer" from Benjamin Rush's book of 1784. Note: if you're thinking about trying rum with pepper, it's not all that great. *Public domain.*

becomes sober. We would like to have the man who refuses to give his wife a just share of his wages, in order that [he] *may waste it on drink, compelled by law to account for what he receives. We would like to have men who have been convicted of drunkenness compelled to show a permit before liquor would be sold to them, and every saloon keeper who sells liquor to a man evidently drunk, heavily fined or his license recalled; many statutes have been enacted the most wise provisions which could be adopted by all. But as long as reformers are intemperate in their means of checking an evil they weaken and hinder the cause of morality.*

Stevens ends his article with an astute observation: "There is such a thing as too much zeal in a good cause."

That the majority of Oregon voters opposed prohibition was demonstrated in 1887, when activists managed to get a prohibition amendment on the ballot. The amendment was soundly defeated, with the ratio of no to yes votes being over two to one.

But Karl Marx was correct in his assertion that technology is the ultimate determinant of a society's morals, and advances in the late nineteenth and early twentieth centuries changed the equation with respect to alcoholic versus nonalcoholic beverages. Modern urban water systems provided safe water from the tap, and pasteurization was successfully applied to fruit juices as well as milk. Machine-made bottles debuted in 1903, enabling these beverages to be inexpensively packaged, and advances in refrigeration meant they could be kept fresh after the bottle was opened. George Welch, who'd begun aggressively marketing his father's pasteurized grape juice during the 1890s, borrowed one of the WCTU's slogans and altered it: "The lips that touch Welch's are all that touch mine." The product soon became so ubiquitous that its more religious consumers were able to convince themselves that it was what Jesus drank, ignoring the fact that grape juice begins to ferment as soon as the grapes are crushed and the juice comes in contact with yeast residing on the skins.

The mechanization of agriculture reduced the physical demands on farmers, and unionization brought more reasonable hours to factory workers. Additionally, the percentage of the workforce engaged in white-collar work increased, and the overall effect was to reduce the number of men who drank to dull the aches and pains that resulted from a long day of hard physical labor. An increasing number became prohibition advocates, many joining the Anti-Saloon League, a mostly male organization founded in the 1890s. The ASL's contribution to the cause was the local option referendum, whereby a state could allow individual counties to vote themselves dry. An Oregon chapter of the ASL was founded in 1903 and got the local option on the summer 1904 ballot. It passed (52 percent in favor), and in the autumn election six counties went dry. By 1910, the number had risen to twenty-three.

But most of the country was still wet, and a lot of men continued to overindulge. Wives were fed up with the amount of time and money their husbands spent in saloons and even more fed up with the way they behaved when they got home. American women pursued a straightforward agenda: first, get the vote, and second, outlaw liquor.

In 1912, Oregon's women got the vote, with 52 percent of the then all-male electorate in favor of it. Oregon's prohibitionists promptly began working on a prohibition amendment, while the WCTU was busily registering women voters. In the 1914 election, the amendment passed, with 136,842 votes in favor and 100,362 opposed. The following year, the state legislature passed the Anderson Act, which outlawed the manufacture and sale of all alcoholic beverages. The new law took effect on January 1, 1916, ending Oregon's first era of winemaking.

6

CHIARO DI LUNA

T he Anderson Act included a provision that allowed Oregon's residents to order alcoholic beverages from out of state. There were limits on this; an order could be placed only once per month, and the quantity was limited to two quarts of distilled spirit or wine or six quarts of beer. Placing wine in the same category as distilled spirits was a weird echo of the 1847 licensing law and again was probably a manifestation of bias against the part of the population who drank wine. That wine drinkers were a minority is shown by the orders placed during 1916: 42,246 quarts of beer, 14,584 quarts of distilled spirits and 343 quarts of wine (of which 72 were for sacramental purposes).[91] This provision was eliminated by a November ballot referendum (51 percent voting for it).

American wine drinkers of the era fell into two disparate groups. The first was wealthy folk of the "old money" variety, those who'd had some exposure to European customs and even some intermarriages with British aristocracy. (Self-made millionaires of the time, on the other hand, were more likely to drink bourbon with their meals.) In Portland, these people (perhaps 1 percent of the population) were supplied during Prohibition by the organization operated by Bobby Evans, who ran a large network of smugglers, moonshiners and bootleggers. Allied with corrupt mayor George Baker and equally corrupt police chief Leon Jenkins, the Evans organization supplied the mayor's well-heeled friends with scotch whiskey and other imported spirits; presumably, this included imported wine for those who wanted it.

The other demographic that drank wine was the immigrant population from countries where wine was simply a beverage taken with meals (exactly what Benjamin Rush recommended). Italians were the largest group of these, with nearly 4 million arriving between 1887 and 1916, the peak period being from 1901 to 1910. Most settled in the East, but some took the train to the West Coast. Oregon saw its Italian-born population increase from 1,014 in 1900 to 5,538 in 1910,[92] and by 1917 there were an estimated 10,000 Italians living in the Portland area.[93] (This figure probably includes the immigrant's American-born children.)

Prior to Oregon prohibition, most Italian Americans in Portland were probably buying inexpensive California Zinfandel. The two quarts of wine allowed per month during 1916 would have been no more than a four-day supply for an Italian family, and it's unlikely many bothered to order any. Instead, a number of home winemakers hoped they could take advantage of a new federal rule that allowed them to make two hundred gallons per year for home use and so purchased grapes from California and turned them into wine. Unfortunately, local law enforcement believed state law took precedence and arrested the home winemakers anyway.[94]

Despite this, many continued to make wine in their basements, a tricky operation because the space had to be ventilated (to avoid a lethal build-up of carbon dioxide gas during fermentation) and because winemaking isn't exactly an odorless activity. A cop on the beat—or an informant—could smell the fermenting wine and track it to a specific house, and with these home winemakers not being part of the Evans network, a visit from the Portland Police Department soon followed.

Floyd Marsh, who was head of the Portland PD vice squad during the 1920s, later wrote:

> *The poor working class of the Italian people, unable to pay off the authorities, were the ones arrested and prosecuted. This gave the publicity that showed Prohibition was being enforced. Here is an instance that is hard to believe: I was given a search warrant to serve on the residence of an Italian widow with three small children. In the basement I found a 10-gallon keg of wine she had made from grapes grown in her backyard. I let the widow stay home on her recognizance to appear in court the following day. Meantime, I received a call from her stating that one of her children was sick and that she would be unable to appear in court on this particular day. When the widow's case was called, I explained to the Court the circumstances, and the judge remarked that he would like to put the*

2390 GALLONS OF WINE SEIZED AND 12 ITALIANS HELD

Wine Presses, Vats and Grapes Gathered in by Police in an Early Morning Raid in City.

FEDERAL FINES ARE FACED

Revenue Officers Will Demand Toll After Prosecution of Cases in the Municipal Court.

Wails rent the air early this morning when Officers Rex and Wright made visits to the homes of 12 Italians and seized 2390 gallons of Italian grape wine.

Besides this, they seized several wine presses, vats, 60 quarts of home-made beer and about a carload of grapes.

At one place the officers found a concrete vat built in the basement, capable of holding several hundred gallons. At another home an old-fashioned screw press was found; around which was worn a hard path, showing that someone had walked about the press many, many times to squeeze the juice from the grapes.

Following is the report of the officers: Andrew Lawrence, 6410 Fifty-ninth street, 100 gallons; John Monaco, 5515 Fifty-ninth avenue, 250 gallons and vat; Sam Tarintino, 5609 Sixty-third avenue, 200 gallons wine and 100 gallons pulp; M. Gasper, 6324 Fifty-eighth street, 200 gallons wine; Vick Carlick, 6335 Fifty-eighth street, 150 gallons; Edward Gio-

nett, 5504 Woodstock avenue, 250 gallons, wine press, vat and 60 quarts home-made beer; Pete Perick, 5515 Sixty-third street, 140 gallons; Sam Cimbolo, 5735 Sixty-third street, 200 gallons; Rafaeli Marccone, 5724 Fifty-ninth avenue, 200 gallons; Fiore Damico, 5735 Fifty-ninth avenue, 200 gallons, press, 80 boxes old grapes; Matt Ektirovich, 6424 Fifty-seventh street, 100 gallons; Dominic Cablato, 5815 Sixty-fifth avenue, 400 gallons.

All have been charged with violation of the prohibition law. After the police department and municipal court have prosecuted these cases, the internal revenue collector then has the power to collect revenue taxes and penalties.

Besides losing 1834 gallons of wine, S. Pieretti, 405 East Market street, and D. Barbagli, 407 East Market street, may have to pay fines amounting to $1000 each. Thursday afternoon each was fined $50 in the municipal court on a charge of violation of the prohibition law. Pieretti was assessed a revenue tax of $600 Thursday, and it is understood that later may be fined in addition to the tax for violation of the federal law. Barbagli is to have his trial in the federal court later.

CRISIS IN GERMANY GATHERING HEADWAY

(Continued from Page One)

unable to agree on a program. They are said to admit that the army can do nothing to save the situation, although they are still claiming that the Hindenburg program will prevent any invasion of Germany by the allied forces. And they are said to be doing everything possible to prevent movement toward an armistice on the military terms which President Wilson has said were the only ones on which a cessation of hostilities was possible.

The degree of their success, however, will depend on whether the commanders in the field are able to continue to withdraw their forces with the comparatively small losses that have marked the retreat to date. And military experts here today said that they saw indications that this will be impossible and that the German military losses from

Article from the *Oregon Daily Journal*, October 18, 1918. Interestingly, five of the "Italians" have non-Italian surnames. *Public domain.*

officer (meaning me) in jail for failing to enforce the Prohibition laws. Such instances hastened my departure from the Vice Squad and the enforcement of Prohibition.[95]

Occasionally, one of these hapless winemakers was fortunate enough to get a lenient judge. One such lucky individual was Louis Dellsilva, whose case was reported in the December 29, 1921 issue of the *Oregon Daily Journal*: "Louis Dellsilva, Italian wine maker, was fined $25. The court imposed the nominal fine because Dellsilva was manufacturing the beverage for his own use."[96]

Little changed in Oregon with the advent of national Prohibition in 1920. The Volstead Act, the Eighteenth Amendment's enforcement enabling legislation, contained a peculiar clause concerning home winemaking. This was Section 29, Title II, which reads:

The penalties provided in this chapter against the manufacture of liquors without a permit shall not apply to a person manufacturing cider and fruit juice exclusively for use in his home, but such cider and fruit juices shall not be sold or delivered except to persons having permits to manufacture vinegar.

This clause was, in fact, a tacit exemption for home winemaking, a fact admitted by those who wrote the act. This admission came from even those who advocated Prohibition, such as Andrew Volstead himself.[97] The wording of the clause was, however, intolerably vague for some, and a 1923 court case forced the issue. The final ruling was that homemade wine and cider were "nonintoxicating in fact" and therefore exempt from the law.[98] The IRS's Bureau of Prohibition was perfectly okay with this; underfunded (agents were woefully underpaid) and understaffed (for example, only eight agents were assigned to Oregon), the bureau had its hands full pursuing smugglers and illicit distillers and didn't want to bother with home winemakers.

At the national level, the effect was a boom in home winemaking. California viticulturalists added acreage and doubled production between 1920 and 1927,[99] shipping over seventy-two thousand boxcars of grapes to the rest of the country in 1927.[100] Unfortunately, production shifted away from grapes that made good wine to grapes that shipped well, such as Alicante Boushet. So many grapes were being grown that supply eventually exceeded demand, and grape prices collapsed in 1926.

The Volstead Act contained language that allowed states to impose laws more restrictive than the federal ones, so in Oregon, the Anderson Act's total ban on alcoholic beverage production took precedence. Whether you could get away with home winemaking depended entirely on the attitude of local law enforcement.

OREGON'S PRE-PROHIBITION WINEMAKERS RESPONDED to state- and country-wide Prohibition in a variety of ways. Some abandoned the grape entirely: Ernest Reuter, for example, pulled up his vines and replaced them with apple trees and potatoes. Others attempted to continue winemaking, hoping that discreet sales of small quantities of wine would keep them off law enforcement's radar. One such was Frederick Stettler of Mountaindale, whom we met in chapter 4. Stettler was arrested in January 1917 for making and selling wine. In April, the Washington County sheriff dumped over 2,000 gallons of Stettler's wine into a gully, some of which was over ten years old and valued at five dollars a gallon. Stettler was required to pay hefty fines but received no prison time, probably in consideration of his age (sixty-nine). He was permitted to keep 350 gallons for personal use.[101] This proved to be a lifetime supply; Stettler died in July 1919.

In the Rogue Valley, August Petard continued making wine, ostensibly for home use. The zealous members of the local WCTU chapter complained about this, and in 1924 the Petard farm was raided by local law enforcement. Six hundred gallons of barreled and fifty quarts of bottled wine were confiscated. Petard pleaded guilty, and although he had to pay fines, the prison sentence was suspended, much to the chagrin of the WCTU.[102]

More successful at avoiding arrest was the Sandoz family south of The Dalles, who continued winemaking during Prohibition and sold it for one dollar per gallon.[103] Julius Sandoz had ceased making wine when his father died in 1919, but his fiancée Anna Kasberger argued that winemaking was a necessary revenue source, and Julius resumed making wine before their marriage in 1920.[104]

Luigi Comini probably continued to make a small amount of wine; his arrangement with the local Catholic church to supply sacramental wine would have allowed him to obtain a permit to make wine for this purpose.

Others, like the growers in California, grew grapes for home winemakers. In Douglas County, Adam Doerner and his son Adolph found this to be a profitable enterprise; according to Adam's great-granddaughter Shelley Doerner Wetherell, the Doerners made more money selling juice to home winemakers than they did while making wine.[105]

Chapter 3 mentions that the Mathiots kept their vineyard going until the farm was sold in the early 1930s; presumably, they were selling grapes to local home winemakers. That they had to sell out suggests that they weren't making a lot of money at this; the collapse of the grape prices in 1926 was probably a contributing factor, as was the onset of the Great Depression in 1929, which resulted in the failure of millions of farms across the United States.

Oregon grape production nearly doubled from 1,421 tons in 1919[106] to 2,668 tons in 1929.[107] These figures were for all grapes, not for "wine grape production," as has been reported elsewhere.[108] Nevertheless, the demand for grapes destined for the table, jam jar and juice bottle is unlikely to have doubled during this period, so production for home winemaking probably accounts for much of the increase.

Prohibition did not bring the results its advocates sought. There was still beer, wine and liquor available for those who wanted it. What it did bring was organized crime, corruption, inconsistent enforcement and the loss of jobs (not just in the manufacturing of alcoholic beverages, but in ancillary industries such as barrel and bottle making). After 1929, the last effect was particularly salient.

By 1932, most people were fed up with it. That year, Oregon citizens voted to rescind the Anderson Act; the following year, they voted to repeal both Oregon's prohibition amendment as well as the federal amendment. By December 1933, three quarters of the states had ratified the Twenty-First Amendment, which repealed the hated Eighteenth.

Oregon was presented with a huge opportunity. California had ruined its previous advantage by replacing its quality grapes with ones whose only virtue was that they stood up well to shipping; millions of vines would have to be regrafted in order to restore the vineyards to their previous condition. In Oregon, pre-prohibition winemakers had demonstrated that *Vitis vinifera* did, in fact, grow well in the state, with early ripening varieties in the Willamette and late ripening ones in southern Oregon and along the Columbia. The state was in a position to become a leader in the production of fine wine.

But it didn't happen. We examine the reasons why in chapter 8.

7

THE VINE, PART II

The vine, which had been tended for over seventy years by the family that had planted it, was being surrounded by tall weeds and blackberry vines. The new owners of the property had no interest in the vineyard, having acquired the farm for the flat land below the butte.

Over the coming decades, its companion vines failed, smothered by the blackberry vines or robbed of light by the Douglas-firs that soon dominated the hillside.

But the vine endured. It sent its roots deeper into the volcanic soil of the butte and its tendrils up the trunks of the trees. It succeeded where the other vines failed.

Against all odds, the vine survived.

8

FRUIT OF THE VINE...AND THE TREE... AND THE BUSH...

Eighteen years is a long time, enough for a generation of children to grow into adulthood. The generation coming of age during Prohibition received no guidance-by-example on how to consume alcoholic beverages. Those who started to drink during this period did it in defiance of law and typically within a context of revelry. For them beer, wine and spirits became a means to get buzzed and not something treated as a component of a meal. Alcohol became, essentially, a party drug. If anything, this reinforced the perception that alcohol use was an immoral activity, even among those who used it; they were, after all, *trying* to be bad. This was true even among the children of Italian immigrants; many, perhaps even most, did not live in households that made their own wine or had access to it.

Many new drinkers were introduced to alcohol via the cocktail, and the concoctions originating during Prohibition were often intended to mask the taste of moonshine whiskey or bathtub gin (both of which could be vile) and relied on a heavy dose of sweeteners to do it. Soft drinks became a popular choice.

In short, what most younger drinkers wanted was something sweet, with a kick. Sweet wines, which before Prohibition took only 40 percent of the market, now commanded 60 percent.[109] Fortified versions, up to 24 percent alcohol, added extra kick for those who wanted it. The demand for table wine, never all that high in Oregon, was even lower than it had been before, and much of that demand was met by wine from California. Roma Wines of Lodi, which by the late '30s was the largest winery in the world, was available in Oregon supermarkets by mid-1935.[110] The company's Zinfandel-based wines weren't exceptional but were passable *vin ordinaire.*

For any Oregon winemaker considering making table wine from *vinifera*, the experience of Emile Aufranc was instructive. Beginning in 1936, Aufranc began making wine, presumably from his father's old vineyard, which had been planted with Chasselas, Pinot noir and Concord. He advertised his product in the classified section of the *Salem Capital Journal*, the ad consisting of the single line, "Grape wine, European method" (one would hope this meant he wasn't using the Concord). This ad ran until mid-1939, but in mid-autumn it was replaced by "Wine at reduced price. Call at Aufranc Winery. Absolutely selling out."[111] His winery was de-registered at the end of the year.

According to BATF records, Oregon's first post-Prohibition bonded winery was Tualatin Winery in Hillsboro. In 1934, it was producing grape wine, as reported by the *Capital Journal*:

> *With all surplus grapes taken gladly by a winery here, farmers in this district are planning to increase their vineyard acreages. About 7,000 gallons of grape juice is fermenting at the Tualatin Valley winery, and the owner said many more tons of grapes could have been used if they were available.*[112]

"If they were available" suggests there wasn't a large supply of grapes, despite the fact that the grapes acquired by Tualatin were probably the extensively planted Concord. On the other hand, there were huge surpluses of other fruits, and Oregon farmers were looking for profitable ways to dispose of those. By 1937, Tualatin had added blackberry, loganberry (a blackberry-raspberry hybrid) and cherry wine to supplement the Concord (all Oregon-sourced) as well as apple wine made from Washington fruit.[113] In 1938, the company dropped the Concord, cherry and apple wines but added one made from strawberries.[114] Tualatin Valley Winery closed in 1940.

The owner of Tualatin was Louis Herboldt, a viticulturalist who'd developed a new variety of seedless grape in 1928.[115] He'd supposedly grown grapes in Europe and had sixty-five varieties of grapes growing in his Oregon vineyard. It's also been reported that he'd grown grapes in Palestine, and was quoted as stating, "As good wines can be made in Oregon as any place in the world."[116] However, a biography constructed from records at ancestry.com shows him as having been born in 1869 to a German family living in the part of the Turkish Empire that later became Romania, and shows him having immigrated to

Above: French Prairie from the top of "La Butte." *Photo by the author.*

Left: A grape grown in the Mathiot vineyard but not found in Oregon today is Chasselas rose. *Photo by Rosenzweig; published under terms of GNU Free Documentation License. https://commons.wikimedia. org/wiki/Commons:GNU_ Free_Documentation_ License,_version_1.2*

At left, Kent Mathiot, great-great-great-grandson of Jean Mathiot; at right, Brenda Eggert of Champoeg Wine Cellars. *Photo by the author.*

David Hill Vineyards and Winery, where the Reuter family planted vines in the late 1880s and Charles Coury planted in 1966. *Photo by the author.*

Above: The old Doerner winery was the seventh bonded after the end of Prohibition. *Photo by the author.*

Left: Doerner label, probably from the late 1940s. *OWHA collection, donation of Shelley and Mike Wetherell.*

Alc. by Vol. 13 Per Cent
Net Contents
One Half Gallon

MELROSE
(BRAND)
OREGON CLARET
Light Grape Wine

Produced and Bottled by
A. H. Doerner Roseburg, Ore.

Left: A label for one of Hugo Neuman's wines. Probably from the World War II period, when only substandard fruit could be used for wine (and apparently had to say so on the label). *From The Eyrie collection; photo by the author.*

Below: Pinot noir in a Dundee vineyard, last week of August 2018. *Photo by the author.*

Richard Sommer founded HillCrest near Roseburg in 1961 and constructed this building in 1974. The gray board in the upper left once read, "Bonded Winery #44." *Photo by the author.*

Willamette Valley. View east, from Marys Peak. Seven times the area of Napa. *Photo by the author.*

Diana Lett at The Eyrie, circa 1968, pruning young vines. *Courtesy of Diana and Jason Lett and The Eyrie Vineyards.*

David Lett delivers pomace to Steve McCarthy of Clear Creek Distillery, circa 1995. *Courtesy of Clear Creek Distillery and Hood River Distillers.*

Four early Pinots: 1967 HillCrest, 1974 Coury, 1972 Erath, 1975 Tualatin. *From the OWHA collection; photo by the author.*

Pinot gris, a variety introduced to Oregon by David Lett. *Photo by the author.*

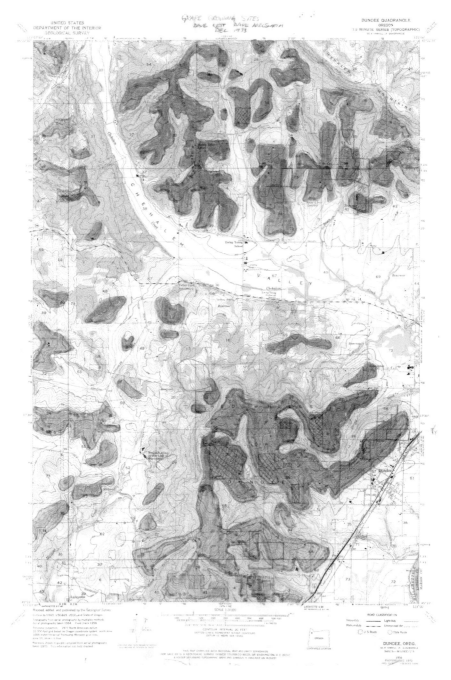

Dundee Quadrangle map, with potential vineyard sites highlighted in pink. *OWHA collection, donation of David Adelsheim.*

Right: Nancy Ponzi "punching down" fermenting grapes, early 1970s. *OWHA collection, donation of Dick and Nancy Ponzi.*

Below: Valley View Winery, August 2018. The haze is smoke from wildfires. *Photo by the author.*

Thin vines from 120-year-old roots. Old vine Zinfandel at The Pines 1852. *Photo by the author.*

Even southern Oregon gets an occasional snowfall. *OWHA collection, donation of Phillipe Girardet.*

Domaine Drouhin Oregon, southwest of Dundee. *Photo by the author.*

Youngberg Hill. This winery and bed-and-breakfast west of McMinnville offers great views to go with your morning coffee. *Photo by the author.*

Amy Wesselman, seen here pouring wine at the 2008 IPNC, was executive director of the International Pinot Noir Celebration from 1999 to 2007. *OWHA collection, donation of the IPNC.*

Sokol Blosser's tasting building, completed in 2013, is powered by solar energy. *Photo by the author.*

Barrel Room at Plaisance Ranch, Applegate Valley. "Plaisance" is the French word for *pleasure*, and it definitely applies here. *Photo by the author.*

Cowhorn in Applegate Valley specializes in Rhone varieties. *Photo by the author.*

The view south from Sarver Winery, west of Eugene. Sarver is a popular weekend spot for the city's wine lovers. *Photo by the author.*

High Pass is one of many small wineries scattered throughout the southwest Willamette Valley. *Photo by the author.*

Harris Bridge Vineyard is a small winery west of Philomath. Its specialty is dessert wine made from Pinot noir and Pinot gris. *Photo by Nathan Warren. Courtesy Harris Bridge Vineyard.*

On a comfortable February 2, 2018, Brenda Eggert of Champoeg Wine Cellars catches up with the latest issue of *Oregon Wine Press*. *Photo by the author.*

Eastern terminus of the Van Duzer corridor, as seen from Van Duzer Vineyards. The haze is smoke from wildfires. *Photo by the author.*

Above: Namasté Vineyards, located in the hills north of the Van Duzer corridor, gets the full benefit of the cool Pacific wind. *Photo by the author.*

Left: Pinot Meunier, Champoeg Wine Cellars. *Photo by the author.*

the United States in 1889 (age twenty), working in Salem in 1895 as a wagon maker, working in Pendleton in 1900 as a blacksmith, marrying Theresa Fuida in 1902 in Idaho, owning a "general" farm in Idaho in 1910 and operating a dairy farm in Hillsboro in 1920 and a "general" farm in 1930. He died 1938, wife Theresa in 1949. They had no children. It's difficult to reconcile the claims made about Herboldt with either the facts of his life or with the operations of Tualatin Valley Winery (as reported in contemporary newspapers). His history and activities as described in modern accounts must have been falsely reported, incorrectly recorded and/or the information became grossly distorted over the years.

The other commercial winery registered in 1933, Sunnybrook Winery of Grants Pass, lasted only two years. In fact, of the forty-two Oregon wineries bonded from 1933 to 1950, thirteen lasted three years or less.[117]

Most of the wineries registered during this period were farm wineries; these paid a lower annual license fee than commercial wineries ($25 versus $250). The newly created Oregon Liquor Control Commission published license fees the first week of February 1934; interestingly, the license for a brewery was the highest ($500), while one for a distillery was only $100. The OLCC was the retailer for distilled spirits in Oregon and remains so to this day.

In early 1936, Albert Kern, a Portland newspaper publisher, proposed a ballot initiative to privatize liquor sales, along with imposing excise taxes and raising license fees. (The distillery license would go from $100 to $2,500.) This elicited a heated response from Hugo Neuman, who operated Willamette Valley Winery southwest of Corvallis. Neuman's letter appeared in the May 11, 1936 edition of the *Capital Journal*:

> [I]*t is just another proposition to put the burden upon the poor man by lessening his chances. How many people got licenses at $100 to make brandy out of prunes that the farmer sold at a loss? Not one farmer, because he could not make it; how then could he pay $2500 for such a license?*
>
> *I have a different plan: To lower the license like they have in other states in order to make it possible to use up all the surplus fruit and not have to give it away for less than it cost to raise it.*
>
> *I am convinced that more wineries in Oregon, lower revenue license, would help the whole state. Oregon is a great fruit state. Fruit is one of its major crops—now let us work for a steady market through the establishment of more wineries.*

Kern and his associates eventually got their proposal onto the ballot (in 1940), but it was defeated, with 77 percent of the electorate voting against it.

Neuman's winery was the third bonded in Oregon after the end of Prohibition. Frustrated with the prices he was getting for his raspberries, loganberries and apples, he began converting the entire crop into wine in 1934.[118] Neuman's was a successful operation; in 1951, he reported average weekly sales of one thousand gallons and earning as much as $35,000 in a three-month period. By this time, he was making grape wine from Concord and White Niagara to supplement his fruit wines. He also turned seventy that year and was ready to retire, expressing regret that none of his seven children wanted to continue the winery.[119] He put the 127-acre farm up for sale in 1961 and died in 1973.

Neuman sold some wine at retail (including by the bottle) but was mostly a wholesaler, selling bulk wine to companies that bottled it and sold it to distributors or retail outlets. The fourth bonded winery in 1934 was probably one such, this being Fred Kraemer of Milwaukie, who listed his occupation in the 1940 Census as "wine merchant." His operation ended in 1948.

Oregon's fifth bonded winery was The Redwoods in Milwaukie, founded by John Broetje, son of the John Broetje who authored a section of *The Grape in Oregon* in 1901. The Broetjes favored native varieties such as Concord and Niagara. The younger Broetje was sixty-nine when he registered his winery in 1933; he died nine years later. He and his wife, Mary, had only one child, Dora, who took over the winery when her father died; the author believes she was Oregon's first female winemaker. Dora Broetje produced Concord, rhubarb, cherry, raspberry and honey wines until the 1960s and still had wine to sell until 1978 when the winery closed.[120] She died in 1982.

The final member of "The Class of '33" was Joseph Lemma & Sons, who operated a department store at Linnton Station in Portland. (For the first three years, the name of the bonded winery was Linnton Department Store.) Lemma probably purchased bulk wine to bottle and sell under his own label. He sold wine until 1940.

The year 1934 saw ten more wineries bonded to operate in Oregon. The first was by Adolph Doerner, who'd been selling juice to home winemakers during Prohibition, near Roseburg. Adolph, unlike his father, did not drink wine, but nonetheless believed it to be a worthwhile business and was the most successful producer of *vinifera*-based wine during this period. He expanded the vineyard to six and a half acres and, in 1941, constructed two new buildings equipped with large concrete tanks.[121] Adam Doerner had originally planted Zinfandel, Riesling and Sauvignon Vert (this might

Storage barrel, old Doerner winery. *Photo by the author.*

actually have been Muscadelle); Adolph added Burger, a white *vinifera* known in France as Monbadon, as well as the hybrid grape Isabella.[122] Doerner bottled two wines under his Melrose label, a "White Grape Wine" (probably a Sauvignon Vert/Burger blend) and an "Oregon Claret" (probably a Zinfandel/Isabella blend). The winery produced as much as 6,900 gallons per year, but the only time demand exceeded production was during World War II. Afterward, demand fell off, and when production ceased in 1953, there were 30,000 gallons in storage (reduced to 13,000 gallons by 1961).[123] Adolph Doerner died in 1964; the remaining wine was sold in bulk and the winery de-registered.

Also registered in 1934 was Endres Winery in Park Place (just north of Oregon City). Henry Endres reportedly started the winery after losing his job. He owned a small farm, planted with three acres of *labrusca* grapes and three acres of orchard (plums, cherries and apples).[124] Henry Endres Sr. operated the winery until his death in 1964, son Henry Endres Jr. until his retirement in 1988. The Endreses made wine from grapes, raspberries, strawberries, plums, honey, loganberry, elderberry and, most famously, rhubarb. The rhubarb wine was reportedly quite strong, both in flavor and alcoholic content, and was popular in the area. The Endres winery also acquired a reputation for selling to underage drinkers; one former customer recalls that when he "was tall enough to see over the counter at Henry Endres Winery I could buy rhubarb wine."

Of the other wineries begun in 1934, only one prompts mention. Heinrich Jaegler, whose farm was near Salem, advertised his wine in the classified section of the *Capital Journal* and always included the phrase "Bring Your Own Jug." After Prohibition, Oregon was one of only six states that permitted retail sales from bulk containers (barrels in those days); prior to Prohibition, most wine was sold that way. Jaegler offered two wines: Concord and a "Dry Burgundy-Reisling." (Yes, that's how he spelled *Riesling*; what exactly "Burgundy-Reisling" was is anybody's guess.) Jaegler sold his wine for about $1.20 per gallon and closed out his operation at the end of 1937.[125]

Six more Oregon wineries were registered in 1935. In Eugene, an ambitious operation was planned by Oregon Wine Industries, which built a plant capable of producing 100,000 gallons per year and employing seven to thirteen people. In fact, only 6,000 gallons of fortified cherry wine were produced during 1936.[126] The company relocated to Portland in 1937 but was out of business by the end of the year.

A farm winery of note was operated by James Kapphan of Salem, who owned a three-and-a-half-acre vineyard planted with Concord from which he produced two to three thousand gallons per year. His first vintage was the 1934, released in June 1935.[127] He began advertising his farm's products in 1937; the first ads read "Wine & Corn Fed Friers," but subsequent ads put the wine and the corn-fed fryers on separate lines, probably because people were showing up at the farm and inquiring about the wine-fed chickens. He ceased production in 1941 but continued selling wine until 1950.

In 1936, at The Dalles, a winery was registered to "Sanders Bros." Robert and Arthur Sanders were cherry growers, and it's a safe bet that their wine was made from cherries. Their property was about a mile east of the old Mesplie vineyard, the one managed by Luigi Comini. There is oral history that Comini was still making wine; Luigi's sons James and Theodore (born in 1931 to Luigi's third wife) state that their "earliest memories" include picking grapes and bringing them to the Mesplie farm for making into wine.[128] After Celia Mesplie Rogers died in 1944, the farm was acquired by the farm's manager Emery Thompson. Thompson continued growing grapes but sold them to Portland-area home winemakers. (Luigi Comini turned seventy-nine in 1944 and was probably no longer making wine; he

Part of an old barefoot-operated grape press, Sandoz farm. *Photo by the author.*

died in 1959.) Thompson sold the property in 1964; the new owner was not interested in growing grapes and abandoned the vineyard.

Celia Rogers's neighbors, the Sandoz family, continued making wine and sold it at their fruit stand. They even added Riesling to the vineyard. The family continued to make wine for personal use after Julius Sandoz died in 1963.[129]

In early 1937, West Hills Winery was registered by Portland businessman Oscar Cooke. The company produced "Blue Concord" wine until 1948.

Later in 1937, Oregon's two commercial distillers got into the wine business. Hood River Distillers, the first post-Prohibition distillery in the state, began producing an apple wine and an apple-loganberry blend. The former was fortified (18–21 percent alcohol) and sweet—just what the post-Prohibition wine drinker wanted. Because of the distillery's high-efficiency column still, during World War II most of its production capability (both fermenting and distilling) was directed toward making industrial alcohol. After the war, the company resumed making wine and continued to do so until 1955.

The other distillery was Columbia Distillers, which registered its winery as Honeywood Distilleries Inc. The company was founded by Ron Honeyman and John Wood; Wood was the company president. In its first year (1937), the new winery produced over forty thousand gallons of blackberry, loganberry and apple wine.[130] By 1938, the wine was being distributed throughout Oregon and to other states as well.[131]

During the war years, production was curtailed by federal fruit allocation policies. Only berries that were "in such condition that they could not be used as food" would be available for wineries.[132] It might be that the resulting reduction in revenue led to insufficient staffing at Honeywood; late in 1942, the OLCC temporarily suspended the winery's license for "unsanitary conditions and with wine that did not meet commission or federal standards."[133]

With the end of the war, Honeywood wasted no time in ramping up production, running ads in September 1945 to recruit workers for its bottling line. The following spring, the company released its first grape wine. Made from Concord, it could be bought at Piggly-Wiggly for seventy-nine cents per bottle.[134] The year 1946 also saw the hiring of a new winemaker, Richard Miller. In 1950, Honeywood began advertising for grapes of "all varieties," offering to pay sixty dollars per ton.[135]

In October 1951, the *Statesman Journal* sent agricultural editor Lillie Madsen and a photographer to the winery for a feature article that appeared in the paper on the eleventh. The pair arrived immediately behind a truck carrying a large load of white grapes. Production manager George Todd informed them the grapes were Riesling from a vineyard near Roseburg. Walter Wood, son of president John Wood, stated, "We take in all the wine grapes produced in southern Oregon and our market would use 10 times the amount we get now." Todd expressed the opinion that there were no finer wine grapes in the United States than those from southern Oregon, with Wood adding, "The grapes of southern Oregon are like those from the

Rhineland." By this time, Honeywood was producing over 200,000 gallons of wine per year; most was still fruit wine, with 400,000 tons of blackberries and loganberries used in 1951.[136]

During the 1950s, the winery introduced a Tokay wine, with some of the grapes sourced from California, as well as a "burgundy" made entirely from California grapes.[137] The manually operated bottling machines were not equal to the task and were replaced with a fully automated system capable of filling over fourteen thousand bottles per day.

John Wood died in 1955. Management of the company apparently suffered, and this, along with declining demand for sweet and fruit wines, led to imminent bankruptcy in 1962. The owners turned to Mary Reinke to take charge; hired as a secretary in 1943, she'd rapidly risen through the ranks and appeared to be the most capable person to run the company. She became president of Honeywood in 1963. By this time, the winery had dropped all of its grape wines except the Concord, a portion of which was made as kosher wine, with Rabbi Yonah Geller of Portland overseeing production.[138]

Returning to the immediate post-Prohibition period, the number of wineries peaked at thirty-one from 1939 to 1941. With this many wineries, there was bound to be some bad stuff, and complaints led to legislation in 1939 to address the issue. The OLCC issued standards for wine quality, and a testing laboratory was created at the agricultural experiment station at Oregon State University. The lab tested wine imported into Oregon as well as wine produced within the state. Farmers producing berries and other fruit destined for wine production were provided with guidance in the sanitary handling of their produce, and in June 1940 the OLCC announced that it had achieved its goal of eliminating "unsound and substandard" wines from the state.[139] The action taken against Honeywood two years later demonstrates the maintenance of quality standards was an ongoing effort.

The number of Oregon wineries fell to twenty-two by the end of World War II, a decline that can be attributed to the demand for berries and other fruit. The number continued to drop, however, bottoming out at six in 1963. These were Honeywood, The Redwoods, Endres, Sweet Home Winery (Hillsboro) and Forrest Berry Farm (Coos County). Doerner's was still on the list; although no longer making wine, it still had plenty to sell.

There are a number of reasons for the decline. First, the fruit surpluses of the 1930s had largely disappeared, with many farmers shifting to crops for which there were agricultural subsidies available. More significantly, tastes had begun to change. The balance of sales was slowly starting to tilt in favor of dry wines and those made from *vinifera* grapes. The process started during the war, when American troops in Europe sampled the local wines and liked them. The 1960s saw a rejection of the blandness and mediocrity that characterized most product categories; people began to realize that there was something better than Roma and Italian Swiss Colony, Folgers and Maxwell House, Budweiser and Miller or even Ford and Chevy.

In 1963, Honeywood was still trying to adapt to this changing environment when management learned that a legislative committee was considering a bill to raise Oregon's excise tax on wine from twenty-three to forty-six cents per gallon. In a press release, George Todd stated this "would seriously aggravate an already critical situation."[140] Mary Reinke spoke to committee members and pointed out that California's tax was only one cent per gallon and Washington's only ten cents, going on to suggest that a tax reduction would be more appropriate. The committee considered a bill to drop the tax to one cent; this was rejected in favor of one dropping it to ten cents. The bill was passed by the Oregon House but failed in the Senate; it was introduced again in 1965 with the same result.[141]

Both years, Honeywood was repeatedly referenced by politicians as Oregon's only winery. This may have been political rhetoric or simple ignorance; in fact, there were six Oregon wineries authorized by the BATF to operate in 1963 and seven in 1965. The latter list included two new ones: HillCrest and Harry & David, both in Douglas County. Harry & David was a fruit company, and its wines were probably made from pears.

HillCrest, on the other hand, was something different. Registered by Richard Sommer in 1961, the property was planted with *Vitis vinifera* vines obtained in northern California. Sommer was, in fact, the first person since Jean Mathiot to come to Oregon for the purpose of making wine from *vinifera* grapes, and his story more properly belongs in the next chapter.

It's easy to express disdain for the fruit wines made in Oregon during the post-Prohibition period, but to do so is to ignore the historical context of these wines. In fact, they were the product of a rare and happy convergence of high supply and high demand; Oregon's growers were producing too much fruit, and consumers were buying the sweet, fruity wines made from this surplus (particularly those wines with an added dollop of brandy). Farming being a low-margin business, to survive, farmers must plant crops for which there is a good market. In the 1930s, the demand for fruit wines drove the production of these, just as today's market demands wine made from the better varieties of *vinifera* grapes. Here in Oregon, the current demand for Pinot noir is driving ever-increasing acreage of it, so much so that the variety is often being planted in unsuitable sites. Were its popularity to diminish, growers would replace it with something else.

Oregon's fruit wines sold well and if not ideal for fine dining, were popular for casual drinking, especially at parties. The March 3, 1960 edition of the *Statesman Journal* describes one held by the state's Republican Party:

> *The whole party was in the Hawaiian motif. Island-type food, souvenirs, table decorations, etc. Men sported Hawaiian shirts and women showed in their mu-mus. And in the midst of all this political poi, shredded coconut and hula music, guess what? The table wine was good old Oregon Loganberry.*

REGARDING PINOT NOIR

Since 1965, Oregon winemaking has been progressively focused on a single variety, Pinot noir. The state's wine industry's growth is due to its achievements with this grape and wouldn't have been as successful without it. A number of white wine grapes do well here (Pinot gris, Pinot blanc, Chardonnay, Riesling and Gewürztraminer), but red wines outsell white—and for a winemaking region to achieve respect, it must have a premier red. Even better if the red is one for which demand exceeds supply, and Pinot noir's status as the holy grail of American winemaking during the late twentieth century drove the expansion of viniculture in Oregon in a way that no other grape could have matched.

Central to understanding the Oregon Pinot noir phenomenon is a study of the variety itself, how it got its name, how it reached Oregon and how and where the phenomenon had its genesis.

THE GRAPE

The grape species *Vitis vinifera* exists as two subspecies. The wild ancestral subspecies, *Vitis vinifera sylvestris*, is dioecious (meaning individual plants are either male or female), while the cultivated subspecies, *Vitis vinifera sativa*, is a hermaphrodite and able to self-pollinate. This mutation has traditionally been believed to have occurred in Transcaucasia, the expanse of land between the Black and Caspian Seas. Evidence for this is both genetic (a high degree of diversity among the grapes of the region) and archaeological. A study conducted in the early twenty-first century, however, revealed that the mutation occurred in *at least* one other place, somewhere in the western Mediterranean region.[142] Subsequent research identified a third genetic group originating in the Balkans/Eastern European area.[143]

Pinot noir is thought to be no more than one generation removed from one of these ancestral strains of *sativa*—perhaps the result of a crossing with some wild vine growing in the area today known as Burgundy. No parent grape for Pinot noir has ever been identified, but it is itself the parent of numerous other varieties. Crossings with the undistinguished but equally ancient grape Gouis yielded Chardonnay, Gamay noir, Aligoté, Melon de Bourgogne and a dozen others.[144]

The antiquity of Pinot noir has given time for many mutations; the best known are Pinot blanc, in which the two genes that control pigment production are inactivated,[145] and the two chimeric mutations, Pinot gris (Pinot blanc cells surrounded by a Pinot noir skin) and Pinot Meunier (Pinot noir cells surrounded by a skin of unknown origin).[146] Even within the Pinot noir variety itself there is a good deal of genetic diversity; vineyards in Burgundy display distinct variations in morphology among the vines. Over fifty strains ("clones") of Pinot noir are officially recognized in France, as opposed to only twenty-five for Cabernet Sauvignon.[147] (There are also another three hundred or so unofficial clones of Pinot noir).

Pinot noir is not an easy grape to grow or vint. The vine is susceptible to powdery mildew and the grapes to bunch rot and, because of its early bud break, is more vulnerable to a late frost than are other varieties. Even in the best of years, yields are low. (The expression is "shy-bearing.") When making wine from it, a gentle touch is required; large destemming machines and pumps that are tolerated by grapes like Cabernet and Syrah can "bruise" Pinot noir. These difficulties have given it something of a bad reputation among growers and vintners. André Tchelistcheff, the mid-twentieth-century dean of California winemaking, is reputed to have said, "God made Cabernet Sauvignon whereas the devil made Pinot noir."[148]

But when it all comes together, the result is a superlative wine. Pinot noir is capable of a graceful elegance that no other grape can match. Depending on the clone used, site conditions, vintage variations and winemaking techniques, the style of Pinot noir wine can range from a light-to-medium-bodied wine characterized by aromas and flavors of red fruits (raspberry, strawberry, cherry, red currant, watermelon) to darker full-bodied wines that suggest blackberry, black cherry and even cassis (that signature element of Cabernet Sauvignon). Wines of the latter type, particularly those from Burgundy, frequently have a "forest floor" or mushroom component, the presence of which helps to distinguish these fuller-bodied Pinots from, say, a Grenache-Syrah-Mourvèdre blend.

THE NAME

The *noir* part is easy—it's the French word for black. The *pinot* part has a more convoluted etymology. The root of the word is *pin*, which is French for pine; the traditional explanation for this association is that a cluster of Pinot noir grapes resembles a pine cone. (This seems a bit of a stretch, but in the absence of any better explanation we'll stick with it.) Some writers have even claimed that *pinot* is French for pinecone; it's not. Pinecone in French is *pomme de pin*, the literal English translation of which is "pine apple" (a confusing asymmetrical translation). The *-ot* suffix is from the Burgundian dialect of French; it's derived from the mainstream French *-et* and its Burgundian form originally had a circumflex over the *o* (as in, *-ôt*). The suffix *-et* (or *-ot*) is a diminutive indicator for masculine nouns; thus, *pinot noir* translates to "black little pine."

It would be nice to end it here, but unfortunately, we can't. About the same time "pinot noir" began appearing in Burgundian documents (late 1300s), someone in the Loire was looking at a cluster of local grapes (the one we now call Chenin blanc) and decided it too looked like a pinecone. Another diminutive-indicating suffix in French is *-eau* (yes, the French word for water), and this grape was dubbed *Pineau de la Loire*. The different spelling was useful; *Pinot* designated the dark grape of Burgundy, while *Pineau* designated the white grape of the Loire. No confusion here.

Unfortunately, this happy state of affairs ended in 1667 when Jean Merlet published a treatise on fruit, *L'abrégé des Bons Fruits*, in which he wrote, "The ordinary black morillon [yet another paranym for Pinot noir] makes better wine. In Burgundy, we call it Pineau."[149] Merlet was apparently considered authoritative, because for the next 250 years, the grape was known as "Pineau Noir" (except in Burgundy, where they continued to use the old spelling). The growers and winemakers in Burgundy wanted the old spelling restored, especially because even native French speakers often mispronounced "Pineau."[150] In 1896, at the winemaker's congress being held in Chalon-sur-

Saone in Burgundy, members voted to make the "Pinot" spelling official. The decision was endorsed and promoted by horticulturalists Pierre Viala and Victor Vermorel, who published the authoritative multivolume reference *Ampélographie—Traité Général de Viticulture* from 1901 to 1910.[151] (Ampelography is the branch of botany concerned with grapevine identification, description and classification.)

The point of this discussion is that until the beginning of the twentieth century *there was no official or universally accepted name for the grape we today call "Pinot noir."* In fact, there have been hundreds of paranyms. As of July 12, 2018, the Wikipedia page "List of grape varieties"[152] lists 318 alternative names for Pinot noir, more than any other variety. (The author's favorite from this list is "Pinot de Migraine.") Only someone unaware of these facts would insist that a nineteenth-century vineyard inventory must contain the exact name "Pinot noir" as a standard of proof for its cultivation in that vineyard.

Two paranyms are relevant to Oregon wine history. The first is "Franc Pinot" (also appears as "Franc Pineau"), which simply means French Pinot and seems redundant, because all Pinot is French. "Franc Pinot" has never been applied to any grape except Pinot noir.

The other paranym of relevance is "Burgunder," which is simply Burgundy in German. Pinot noir is the mostly widely planted red wine grape in Germany, and their name for it is its place of origin. If you had asked, in English, a nineteenth-century English-speaking German grower of Pinot to name the grape, he would have replied, "Burgundy."

CALIFORNIA

Pinot noir might have arrived in California as early as the 1850s, but there is no firm evidence for it. With 105 varieties offered, one would think Antoine Delmas had it in his nursery, but there is no record of him advertising it. Charles Lefranc may have planted some in his father-in-law's vineyard but wasn't advertising any for sale. The first to do so was Agoston Haraszthy in 1862, following his collecting expedition to Europe. The first grower and vintner of record is Jean-Baptiste Portal, who founded Burgundy Vineyard in 1872. Located west of San Jose, the winery was producing a blend of Pinot noir, Poulsard and Malbec.[153] Antoine Delmas's son Delphin started a winery in 1882 and was growing Pinot noir, along with

Charbono, Carignane, Zinfandel and Chasselas.[154] Hiram Crabb, founder of the famous To-Kalon vineyard in Napa Valley, listed "Pinot noiren" in his 1882 catalogue. (He also sold Mondeuse under the name "Black Burgundy," which must have confused a number of buyers.)[155]

There was little Pinot noir planted in California before Prohibition. Eugene Hilgard, a professor of agricultural chemistry at the University of California–Berkeley and director of the State Agricultural Experiment Station, conducted a study of Pinot vines planted at various experiment station sites. Several different variants (what we today call "clones") were planted; their names were probably those given by the nurserymen who sold them to the researchers. These were "Blauer Burgunder," "Franc Pinot" and "Pinot Noiren" (also included was "Pinot de St. George," which was actually Négrette); the test planning locations were Fresno, Mission San Jose, Cupertino, Tulare, Paso Robles and Amador Station. Results were not encouraging, and in 1894 Hilgard wrote:

> *Under conditions of wine-making in California, it is next to impossible to make and keep a perfectly sound wine of Pinot alone. In some locations it is doubtless possible to make a Pinot wine of high quality and to age it, but only with minute attention to detail and elaborate care, which no price that is likely to be obtained at present would justify.*
>
> *For the hot interior localities the Pinots must be unhesitatingly rejected. In the cooler localities of the Coast Range they may be utilized by blending in the fermenting-vat with some more acid and more robust variety.*[156]

The largest pre-Prohibition commercial plots were at Beaulieu and Inglenook, and some vintages of these turned out well (probably cooler years). An 1892 Inglenook was opened in the late 1940s and found to be "delicate, fruity and undeniably pinot."[157]

After Prohibition ended, there was increased interest in Pinot noir, but it still wasn't widely planted. The most significant planting, from the perspective of finding the best locations for it in California (and also significant to the variety's history in Oregon), was that done by Louis Martini in the cool Los Carneros region. Begun in 1946, by the 1950s this Pinot vineyard was seventy acres in size.[158]

CLONES

All cultivated grapevines are clones in the sense that all originated as cuttings from a parent vine. Different vines of the same variety can have different characteristics, and cuttings that originated from the same vine or group of vines are given a specific designation to distinguish them from cuttings taken from another source; viticulturalists refer to these selections as "clones." In the United States, these designations are assigned by an organization known as Foundation Plant Services. Created at UC Davis during the late 1950s (known then as Foundation Plant Materials Services), FPS acquires, tests, treats (if necessary), designates and distributes grapevines (also plums, pistachios, strawberries, sweet potatoes and roses). The designations originally used "FPMS," followed by an alphanumeric code (for example, "FPMS 1A") but in 2003 switched to "FPS" ("FPMS 1A" becoming "FPS 1A"). Many writers substitute "UCD" (for University of California at Davis) for FPMS/FPS, but this is imprecise because for a while the university's viticulture department had its own numbering scheme.

The first three Pinot noir clones certified by FPS were FPMS 1A, 2A and 3A. These were sent to UC Davis in 1952 from Wädenswil, Switzerland, and were tagged "Blau Burgunder" ("Blue Burgundy"), the Swiss name for Pinot noir. The "Wädenswil clones" were certified in 1962; 1A and 2A are still available in 2018; 3A was de-certified in 1981 when it was discovered to be infected with leafroll disease.[159]

The next to be certified were the "Pommard clones," FPMS 4, 5 and 6, which originated in the Pommard district of Burgundy. FPMS 4 was the original cutting and was certified in 1963. FPMS 5 and 6 were the result of "thermotherapy" (a.k.a. "heat treatment") applied to FPMS 4, this consisting of growing the vine in hothouse conditions in order to eliminate viruses. FPMS 5 and 6 became available in 1967. In 1980, all three tested positive for "Rupestris Stem Pitting" disease and were decertified.[160]

There was also "Gamay Beaujolais," what FPMS thought was Gamay noir, the preferred red wine grape in the southern part of Burgundy. It 1974, it was discovered to be Pinot noir and was moved to that list.

These six (or seven, if you include the "Gamay Beaujolais") were the only certified selections available before 1974. There were, of course, selections available from commercial vineyards, such as the Martini vines in Carneros (heat-treated versions of which became FPMS 13 and 15 in 1974). Many other clones have been certified since then; we'll defer discussion of these until they become relevant.

OREGON

When Jean Mathiot went on his vine-buying trip to California in 1858, the varieties at the top of his list were probably Pinot noir, Poulsard and Chardonnay; unfortunately, these were not available, even at Delmas's well-stocked nursery. The following year, son Adolphe had no better luck; Pinot noir was not available until 1862, Poulsard not until the 1870s and Chardonnay not until the 1880s. They acquired instead Pinot Meunier, Black Muscat and Chasselas and, if Adam Shipley's report is accurate, forty-seven other varieties (probably in smaller quantities).

The first documented Oregon Pinot noir grower would have been Peter Britt, whose son Emil's journals record the planting of "Frank pinot" in 1887.[161] It's doubtful the Britts planted a lot of it; the Rogue Valley is not an ideal place for Pinot noir, and most of what they produced probably ended up in blends.

Adolph Reuter, responding to the query sent by E.R. Lake for his 1901 paper "The Grape in Oregon," wrote, "I find Sweetwater, Zinfandel, Burgundy, Black Hamburg, Muscatel, Red Mountain, Chasselas Fountainbleu [sic], Deleware [sic], and Muscat excellent for our purposes." Reuter was German, and to him, "Burgundy" was the name of the grape. Chapter 4 mentions that the Reuters received a bronze medal for their Burgundy at the 1901 Exposition in Buffalo, New York, but it's unknown if this was a pure varietal bottling or a blend.

August Aufranc, also responding to Lake, listed White Chasselas, Red Burgundy and Concord. The "Red" qualifier for Burgundy is confusing; Pinot noir is blue-black. Pinot Gris is red, but that grape did not reach North America until the twentieth century. It might be a reference to the color of the wine, in the same way the Hilgard article referenced earlier was titled "Red Burgundy Type."

None of these Pinot plantings survived; Britt's son did not continue viticulture and probably converted the land to pasture. Ernest Reuter converted his vineyard to apple and potato production at the onset of Prohibition, and when Aufranc's son Emile died in 1943, the farm was sold (neither of his sons went into farming). It's unlikely the new owner was interested in viticulture. Nevertheless, these three were growing Pinot noir in Oregon over sixty years before anyone else. Peter Britt, not Richard Sommer (**MYTH NUMBER SEVEN**), was the first to grow it in Oregon, and Frederick Reuter, not Charles Coury or David Lett (**MYTH NUMBER EIGHT**), was the first to grow it in the Willamette Valley.

Page from Emil Britt's vineyard diary. Entry 20 is a duplication from the previous page, where it appears as "Frank pinot." This page is used because it shows the source as being Louis Rothermel of San Jose. *Courtesy of Southern Oregon Historical Society.*

But Britt's, Reuter's and Aufanc's plantings were temporary; in fact, it's useful to think of these growers as the Vikings of Oregon Pinot noir production. Leif Ericson might have reached North America five hundred years before Christopher Columbus, but the Vikings didn't stay for more than a generation or two. Columbus, on the other hand, initiated a wave of migration that continues to this day.

So, who was the Columbus of Oregon Pinot noir? Richard Sommer was unquestionably the first to grow it after Prohibition, planting it at his HillCrest Vineyard in the early 1960s. Sommer was a 1957 graduate of the University of California at Davis, majoring in agronomy. In those days, the viticulture professors at UC Davis imparted the wisdom that most of California was too warm for Pinot noir, yet if asked about Oregon would declare it too cold for any variety of *vinifera* to ripen. Of course, anyone who's visited southwest Oregon knows it's not that different from northern California, but the faculty at UC Davis apparently believed Oregon was covered in glaciers and swarming with polar bears. There were probably a number of students who had doubts about the accuracy of their professors' pronouncements, but Sommer was the first to act on them.

After graduating, Sommer moved to Jackson County, Oregon, where his uncle and widowed mother lived. His uncle owned a fruit farm, and Sommer tended the property's vineyard. In 1959, he obtained vine cuttings from the Louis Martini property in Carneros, which he planted in a temporary vineyard in southern Douglas County. The varieties were Riesling, Pinot noir, Gewürztraminer, Chardonnay, Cabernet Sauvignon and Sauvignon blanc. He spent his spare time driving around Jackson and Douglas Counties looking for a place to start a vineyard. In Douglas County, he met the Doerners, who helped him with his property search.[162] He spent some time working in the Doerner vineyard[163] and made some wine from their grapes. He moved to Roseburg in 1960, taking a job with the county assessor's office, and narrowed his search to Douglas County.

In 1961, Sommer acquired a forty-acre former chicken farm located about two miles southwest of the Doerner property. The property was on top of a plateau overlooking Elgarose Creek Valley, about 850 feet above sea level. His initial vineyard comprised three and a half acres planted with Riesling, Pinot noir, Chardonnay, Cabernet Sauvignon and Gewürztraminer. Additional Riesling planted in 1962 and 1963 doubled the size of the vineyard, and more Pinot noir and Riesling planted in 1964 brought it to ten acres.[164]

Sommer's first production was two hundred gallons of Riesling in 1963; by 1966, production was up to six thousand gallons. In 1967, he released Oregon's first varietal labeled Pinot noir, the same year he quit his day job to concentrate on winemaking. His most popular wine of the 1960s was "Mellow Red," an off-dry blend of Riesling and Cabernet Sauvignon, which, in its early days, contained some elderberry as well. His showcase varietal bottling was Riesling, and many were excellent. In 1975, he built a new ten-thousand-square-foot winery. He continued to add acreage (twenty in cultivation by the late 1970s, eventually reaching fifty) as well as varieties, planting a total of thirty-five different grapes. (Most were in small experimental plots.) Of the thirty-five, all but one were from California; the exception was Zinfandel, started from Doerner vines dating from the late 1880s. The Zinfandel did not work out, and he phased it out at the end of the 1970s. By the end of the 1980s, his annual production had reached thirty thousand gallons and he was distributing outside of Douglas County.[165]

Sommer turned seventy-three in 2002, by which time managing the vineyard and winery was becoming a challenge for him. The following year, he sold HillCrest to Dyson DeMara, the current owner. Sommer died in 2009 at age seventy-nine.

Richard Sommer, founder of HillCrest Winery. *Courtesy of Douglas County Museum.*

It's tricky assessing Sommer's place in the history of Oregon winemaking. He was unquestionably a pioneer, establishing a vineyard in Oregon when conventional wisdom considered this folly. He was the first Oregon grower of the modern era to plant Pinot noir and the first ever in the state with a varietal bottling of it. He introduced fermentation in stainless-steel tanks and, with Paul Bjelland, founded the Umpqua Grape Growers Association (which, after a series of name changes, merged with a similar Willamette Valley group to become the Oregon Winegrowers Association). Particularly after he became better known, he provided encouragement and expertise to others starting wineries in Oregon, especially in the southern part of the state.

Was Sommer's production of Pinot noir at HillCrest Winery the genesis of the Oregon Pinot noir phenomenon? The historical record does not support that conclusion; the wineries that raised Oregon Pinot noir to prominence were located in the northern Willamette Valley, with the first being those started by David Lett and Charles Coury. According to Lett, he and Coury were unaware of Sommer and had "already rejected southern Oregon in theory as too warm."[166] It's also important to understand that Sommer's efforts were focused on Riesling. (Bill Nelson, a consultant who worked with Sommer in the early 1970s, characterizes HillCrest as "primarily a Riesling operation with a little bit of Cabernet Sauvignon.")[167] It's a stretch to believe that a modest planting of Pinot noir in southern Oregon inspired anyone to start a winery in the Willamette and devote most of their efforts to that variety. As we will see, the Oregon Pinot noir phenomenon had a different genesis, one totally independent of Sommer and HillCrest.

THE WILLAMETTE VALLEY

Among those studying viniculture at UC Davis in the early 1960s were Charles Coury and David Lett. Charles Coury was born in New Jersey in 1931, but his family had moved to Los Angeles by the time of the 1940 Census. In 1952, he received a degree in climatology from UCLA, after which he served in the U.S. Navy from 1953 to 1956. After resuming civilian life, he got into the wine retail trade, an occupation that kindled an interest in viniculture. He enrolled in the UC Davis enology program, pursuing a master's degree. His master's thesis, "Wine Grape Adaption in the Napa Valley, California," dealt with the various models used to choose the best locations for grape varieties. Coury favored the model that matched a variety's maturation period with an area's growing season, rejecting the traditional California view that a long growing season was acceptable for any type of grape, with early ripening varieties simply being harvested sooner. He presented data showing that in France, variety "adaption" (the grapes doing better than in other locations) occurred in regions where the growing season matched the grape's maturation period, and postulated his "Hypothesis of Cold Limit Amelioration," to wit:

> *Any variety yields its highest quality wines when grown in such a region that the maturation of the variety coincides with the end of the growing*

84

season. Or another way of expressing the concept: Any variety yields its highest quality wines when grown in a region whose ecologic potential to mature fruit just equals the requirements of the variety, no more or no less.[168]

A problem with the hypothesis, at least in terms of real-world applicability, is that the published length of a region's growing season is an *average* generated from many years of records. Two different regions might have the same average growing season, but one might have significantly higher year-to-year variability of weather and will therefore suffer a higher percentage of poor vintages. This is a challenge for both Willamette and Burgundy growers, where variations in weather—and therefore vintage—are greater than for Pinot-friendly locales in California.

Charles Coury's thesis references Victor Pulliat, whose 1888 paper presented the same argument in favor of matching maturation periods to growing seasons. Pulliat devised a five-category classification system for grape maturation periods indexed on Chasselas; those that ripen before Chasselas are "Early Ripening," those that ripen at the same time as Chasselas are "First Period" and so on. (Pinot noir is First Period.) Also referenced in Coury's paper was Albert Winkler, a mid-twentieth-century UC Davis viticultural researcher who assigned grapes to categories based on the number of "heat units" (today usually called Growing Degree Days) a variety needs to reach maturation. Because average GDDs are a common metric used in characterizing the climate of a place, Winkler's system seems more precise at matching a variety of grape to its ideal locations.

Lett, Coury and their classmates were all familiar with Pulliat and Winkler and would have discussed their ideas. These discussions would have included application of the cold limit amelioration hypothesis to a number of grape varieties, including Pinot noir, and to a number of regions, including Oregon.

Coury received his master's degree in absentia; by that time (June 10, 1964), he was living in the Alsace district of France, studying local winemaking.

Coury's classmate David Lett was born in Chicago in 1939. By 1946, his family was living near Salt Lake City, where he attended the University of Utah and majored in premed and philosophy, graduating in 1961. In early 1962, he applied to a dentistry school in San Francisco; driving back to Utah from an admission interview, he learned that the highway's pass through the mountains was closed. Lett decided to take a side trip to Napa Valley, where he visited Lee Stewart's winery, Chateau Souverain. Stewart's passion for winemaking was infectious, and Lett decided he'd prefer it to dentistry. He applied and was accepted to the UC Davis viticulture program and spent the next two years there. While there, he sampled some good Burgundy and decided it was the kind of wine he wanted to make. Lett received a bachelor's degree in January 1964, after which he left for France to visit its vineyards and wineries. While there, he visited the University of Dijon, where he met Dr. Raymond Bernard, one of France's top viticultural experts.

Nine months later, Lett was back in California collecting cuttings, and he had three thousand by the end of January 1965; his collection included Pinot noir, Chardonnay, Riesling, Gewürztraminer and "Gamay Beaujolais." He arrived in the central Willamette in early February and leased some land just east of Corvallis to use as a nursery. He began planting on February 22 and was done on March 1. Three hundred vines ordered from FPMS arrived on March 13; these included Pinot Meunier, Pinot Gris, Muscat Ottonel, Petite Syrah and "Pinot blanc" (another misidentified grape, which later turned out to be Melon de Bourgogne). He planted these the next day with help from Charles Coury, who'd recently returned from Alsace.

In April, Lett planted some vines for Coury, one-year-old rootings that Coury had sent up from California.

Coury and Lett briefly shared an apartment in Silverton. Using that as their home base, they drove around the valley looking for vineyard sites. Coury purchased his first, in September, near Forest Grove. The property was, in fact, the same on which the Reuters had been raising *Vitis vinifera* some fifty years before. Shortly after buying it, Coury met two of Ernest Reuter's sisters (he had five, born between 1879 and 1890), who told him about Ernest's silver medal in the 1904 St. Louis World's Fair.[169] In early 1966, Coury began moving his vines from Lett's nursery to the Forest Grove vineyard, and he and his wife, Shirley, moved into the property's one-hundred-year-old farmhouse.

With his cuttings rooting and with rent to pay, David Lett needed a day job to make ends meet. For a while, he worked on a berry farm, but in early 1966 he started selling textbooks for the Scott Foresman Company, continuing his vineyard search in his spare time.

The summer of 1966 saw two major events in Lett's life. One was finding and purchasing the property for his vineyard, a twenty-acre plum orchard in the Dundee hills. The other was meeting Diana Carlsen while attending a Scott Foresman training session in Chicago. Diana, who was from Dallas, was also attending the session, and she and David quickly developed a strong mutual attraction. They married on October 1, 1966, in Dallas, after which they headed to Oregon, where David presented her with her two wedding gifts: an L.L. Bean rain suit and a shovel.[170]

Early February 1965. David Lett has loaded his uncle's horse trailer with vine cuttings and is about to leave for Oregon. *OWHA collection, donation of The Eyrie Vineyards and Jason Lett.*

The young couple began the laborious task of digging up the young vines at the nursery site, transporting them to the Dundee property and replanting them there. On the new property, a pair of red-tailed hawks were nesting in a Douglas-fir, raising a new brood. Watching the birds provided distraction from the tedious work; it also inspired the name of the winery.

10

THE EYRIE

David and Diana Lett finished transplanting their vines in 1967. The 3,300 or so vines covered almost five acres; there was an acre of Chardonnay, an acre of "Gamay Beaujolais," three quarters of an acre of Pinot noir, a half acre of Riesling, with Pinot gris, Pinot Meunier, Gewürztraminer, Muscat Ottonel, Petite Sirah and "Pinot blanc" making up the balance.[171] The Pinot noir was all Wädenswil (FPMS 1A). The Pinot Meunier vines had a more interesting background; FPMS had no certified Meunier selection at that time, and the 37 cuttings sent to Lett were from a vine in a vineyard managed by the Department of Viticulture and Enology. That vine, of unknown origin, was planted in 1950.[172]

Lett's vines had come from a variety of sources. Chardonnay, Riesling and Gewürztraminer came from the Draper vineyard in Napa Valley, Pinot noir and "Gamay Beaujolais" from Wente; there were even cuttings from Gallo. Pinot gris came from the UC Davis school of viticulture, and FPMS supplied Pinot Meunier, Pinot Gris, Muscat Ottonel, Petite Syrah and "Pinot blanc."[173]

Charles Coury had also completed planting his vineyard. His Pinot noir was mostly Wädenswil, but there was also some from an unknown source. It's widely believed that the cuttings were illegally imported by Coury. (Such imports are termed "suitcase clones.") Not only did he plant this selection in his vineyard but he also sold it as "Pommard" from his nursery, along with the actual Pommard clone FPMS 4.[174] Eventually, this mystery selection became known as the "Coury clone."

David Lett was still working for Scott Foresman and traveling around the Northwest. (His territory ranged from San Francisco to Alaska.) Initially, Diana accompanied him on these trips, but after becoming pregnant, she stayed at home. In late 1967, while David was away, a "young, but very tall" Dick Erath paid a visit.[175] Erath was a Californian who'd been making his own wine for a couple of years. Earlier that year, he was taking an enology class at UC Davis, one that Richard Sommer was attending as well. The instructor teaching the course introduced Erath to Sommer, told Erath about Lett and Coury and gave him their addresses. The following autumn, after interviewing for a job with Tektronix in Beaverton, Erath stopped at the Letts' place only to find him away. He had better luck with Coury; the two stayed up until four o'clock in the morning discussing why Coury and Lett had chosen the Willamette Valley for their vinicultural efforts. In the end, Erath was convinced; he took the Tektronix job and made plans to move to Oregon.[176]

Lett continued to expand his vineyard. In 1968, he added another 1.71 acres of "Gamay Beaujolais," 1.23 acres of Chardonnay, .94 acres of Pinot noir and .63 acres of Riesling. The year 1970 saw another 1.8 acres of Chardonnay, 1.6 of Riesling and .3 of "Gamay Beaujolais," bringing total acreage to 12.67.[177]

David and Diana Lett's family was growing as well; their first child, James, was born in 1968, followed by Jason in 1969.

By 1969, the vines were maturing, and it was a safe bet that there would be grapes to harvest the following year. Lett estimated a fully equipped winery would cost $30,000 and sought a loan for it, but for some reason loan officers were uninterested in financing a thirty-year-old's unprecedented project to start a winery in the Willamette Valley. With harvest approaching, Lett was able to rent for $25 per month a twenty-five-by-forty-foot air-conditioned insulated room in the vacated Swift and Co. building in McMinnville. He brought in $2,500 of "mostly makeshift" equipment (including a grape press from Richard Sommer, which probably once belonged to the Doerners) along with thirty new French oak barrels.[178] He registered the winery with the BATF, receiving license BW-OR-49. (Coury had registered his sooner, receiving BW-OR-48.)

Both Coury and Lett made wine in 1970, including Pinot noir. Existing examples of Coury's early bottles usually lack the separate vintage label; The author does not know if this was originally the case or if they just came off. With these bottles, there is no way to tell the difference between a 1970 and a 1973.

Charles Coury's first Pinot noir, from the 1970 vintage. *From the David Hill collection, photo by the author.*

David Lett produced six hundred gallons of Pinot noir in 1970 but was not entirely happy with it. He blended it with a small amount of undisclosed white wine (probably Pinot gris) and labeled it "Spring Wine." The next year's Pinot noir was better, and he produced it as a varietal bottling. "Spring Wine" was bottled for several more years but was an all-white blend from 1971 on.

Although Charles Coury had rejected California as a place to grow Pinot noir, he did not reject California vinicultural methods. He sought to maximize yields and made the wine using what's been called the "standard red wine method." This was a high-intervention style of winemaking, using "fancy crushers, destemmers, and presses,"[179] stainless-steel temperature-controlled fermentation tanks, pumping the wine over the "cap" that develops during fermentation and using centrifuges to clear the wine. He rejected the use of barrels for aging, stating, "People love old oak as a reaction to the automated, mechanical world they live in, but there is a lot of mystique in winemaking using all glass and stainless steel."[180] There are grapes tolerant of this high-technology approach (Cabernet, Zinfandel, Syrah), but Pinot noir is not one of them, and the wine made by Coury won no accolades.

He failed to develop a customer base and, by 1978, was bankrupt, with his vineyard and winery becoming the property of his creditors. Coury went on to pursue an equally unsuccessful career in brewing. He died in 2004.

Although Coury's involvement in Oregon viniculture was brief, his contributions were significant. At UC Davis, he and David Lett bolstered each other's beliefs about Pinot noir and Oregon, and after moving there, they continued to collaborate for a short period. As we see in the next chapter, Coury participated in early initiatives that created a conducive environment for the growth of the Oregon wine industry and gave encouragement and assistance to the other winemakers getting started during the 1968 to 1978 period.

David Lett didn't have the gadgetry that Coury used, and this proved to be a blessing in disguise. Lett used a punch down tool to irrigate the cap while the grapes were fermenting, cleared the wine with minimal filtration and aged the wine in barrels. His traditional techniques were not entirely the result of limited means; in fact, they were right in line with his low-intervention approach to winemaking. The result was better wine, and by the mid-1970s, he was producing world-class Pinot noir.

In 1972, Lett was able to purchase the building that housed his operation. That same year, the *Salem Capital Journal* ran an article on Lett and his winery. The article describes him as "beaming with intellect but curiously resembling the little old wine maker" (a reference to an Italian Swiss Colony television commercial from the 1960s). "The Willamette Valley is almost perfectly adapted to wine production," said Lett, who asserted, "We have a potential to produce better wine than Europe"[181] (a statement eerily similar to ones made seventy years before).

In 1973, Lett was able to quit his job selling textbooks. The following year, FPMS announced the discovery that the "Gamay Beaujolais" it had been distributing was actually Pinot noir; in an instant, Lett's Pinot noir acreage doubled.

The Eyrie winery and tasting room, McMinnville, Oregon. *Photo by the author.*

But the wine-buying public was not yet tuned in to Oregon Pinot; California Cabernet Sauvignon was becoming popular, and Lett, using Washington fruit, began bottling Cabernet Sauvignon and Merlot. He wasn't happy about it, but these bottlings generated needed revenue for The Eyrie.

Over the course of the 1970s, The Eyrie's Pinot noir gained followers; among them was Becky Wasserman, an American living in Burgundy who exported wine to the United States. In 1978, she acquired bottles of Lett's first reserve Pinot, the 1975 South Block. The following year, she decided to submit some to the wine Olympiade being held by the French magazine *Gault-Millau*. Although there are accounts that claim she did this without the Letts' knowledge, Wasserman states that she did, in fact, obtain David Lett's permission.[182]

The particulars of this competition are hazy; the number of wines entered has been reported as 330 and 586 and Lett's Pinot variously reported as having scored in the top ten of the Pinot noir category, or in the top ten overall, or as placing third overall. Whatever its exact finish, it did well enough to attract the attention of prominent Burgundy producer Robert Drouhin, who decided to organize a rematch the following year, pitting a selection of Drouhin's Burgundies against high-scoring Pinots from elsewhere. In the final scoring, The Eyrie wine came in second, behind the 1959 Drouhin Chambolle-Musigny and ahead of the 1961 Drouhin Chambertin Clos-de-Bèze. The results were widely reported in the media, and suddenly Oregon Pinot noir was in the spotlight.

David Lett was elated; he could stop making Cabernet Sauvignon.

Lett also introduced Pinot gris to Oregon. He bottled his first in 1971, from vines that originated as 65 cuttings acquired from FPMS in early 1965 and 160 cuttings from four UC Davis vines.[183] Only twenty-five cases were produced that year and for the next nine years thereafter. In 1979, he decided he wanted to increase production and grafted Pinot gris onto his Riesling vines and, in 1980, added an additional nine and half acres of Pinot gris to his Stonehedge vineyard. Production rose from one hundred cases in 1981 to three thousand in 1984. The wine became progressively more popular; the one hundred cases produced in 1981 took a year to sell, with the three thousand produced in 1984 sold in the same period of time.[184]

Over the years, The Eyrie has added vineyard acreage and additional varieties. When it was discovered that the "Pinot blanc" acquired from FPMS was actually Melon de Bourgogne, the wine was relabeled and bona

Left: The great and the not-so-great. At left, a bottle that once held 1975 The Eyrie South Block Reserve, the wine that defeated all but one Drouhin Burgundy in 1980. At right, a bottle of Coury "Gamay" from the same year FPMS revealed the grape was a variant of Pinot noir. *From the OWHA collection, photo by the author.*

Below: David Lett's supervisor from the textbook company, Menton Sveen, not only gave him a month off for harvest but pitched in as well. Sveen (*left*) and David Adelsheim are pictured here operating the press acquired from Richard Sommer, which came with the advice, "Be sure to wrap a towel around the mechanism, or your Riesling will become Greasling." *Courtesy of The Eyrie and Jason Lett.*

fide Pinot blanc planted. Other additions include Trousseau and that favorite of nineteenth-century Oregon viniculturalists, Chasselas.

David Lett participated in many of the initiatives that were responsible for the success of the Oregon wine industry (more about this in the next chapter) and exerted influence beyond winemaking. Steve McCarthy, founder of the pioneering Clear Creek Distillery, has stated that it was Lett who persuaded him to begin making grappa and supplied him with the pomace (the leftovers from wine production) to make it.[185]

Lett's health began to fail during his mid-sixties, and in 2005, son Jason took over the winery. David Lett died in 2008 at age sixty-nine.

11

ARTISANS OF WINE, ARCHITECTS OF INDUSTRY

Dick Erath and his family moved to Oregon in February 1968. After several months of searching for a potential vineyard site, he purchased forty-nine acres near Newberg. He'd planned to put a mobile home on the property, but the well he'd drilled yielded non-potable water. Fortunately, an old school acquaintance owned a cabin about a mile from Erath's property and invited him to use it. Erath planted four acres of vines in 1969; a little less than half was Pinot noir, with the balance being Riesling, Chardonnay, Gewürztraminer and experimental plantings of twenty-two other varieties.[186] His first vintage was in 1972.

During 1969, Lett, Coury and Erath learned of a nursery in southern Oregon that was obtaining grapevines from a source known to be infected with a virus. Oregon already had a law prohibiting nurseries to sell or store infected material (specifically clause 200 of ORS Chapter 571, passed in 1963), so when the growers alerted the ODA (Oregon Department of Agriculture) about the problem, the agency was able to issue a quarantine on the import of rooted cuttings (this to prevent phylloxera) and require unrooted cuttings be certified as disease-free.[187] A September 2018 download of the ODA's regulations governing importation of plant material showed that these rules are still in effect. (Note: it's been reported elsewhere that the growers "lobbied the legislature" to effect these measures; in fact, the 1963 law provided the ODA with the authority to impose the proposed regulations.)

The growers were seeking sources for healthy vines, and a 1970 meeting with the OSU School of Agriculture Extension Service concluded on an auspicious note; the Extension Service personnel expressed optimism that

Dick Erath with vine cuttings, 1974. *OWHA collection, donation of Erath Winery and Dick Erath.*

by using hothouse techniques they'd be able, within a year, to generate ten thousand cuttings each of Pinot noir, Riesling, Chardonnay and Cabernet Sauvignon. Apparently, there were no funds available for this ambitious project, because nothing came of it.

The newspaper article that describes the meeting does not identify the OSU participants (the growers were listed as Sommer, Lett and Coury), but it's a safe assumption that one of them was Hoya Yang. Yang had arrived from China in 1938 to study food sciences, acquired a doctorate in the subject and joined the OSU faculty in 1956. He was interested in wine production and had conducted studies in the late 1950s to assess the suitability of various grapes for cultivation in Oregon. There were about forty varieties included in these trials, with about a third each of *Vitis vinifera*, native varieties and hybrids. One of the grapes was "Early Burgundy," which might have been Pinot noir, but the lack of any description for this grape prevents a definitive identification.[188]

In 1970, Erath and Coury started a grapevine nursery, introducing to Oregon the Pommard clone of Pinot noir (FPMS 4) and an additional

Wädenswil clone (FPMS 3A). The partnership ended in 1971; Coury continued to operate the nursery for several more years. Both he and Erath (who'd opened his own nursery in 1973) worked with FPMS to obtain newly certified clones; the organization had added a number in 1974. These were the "Mariafeld" clones (FPMS 17 and 23) from Switzerland, one from Germany (FPMS 27), two from the "lost" vineyard in Amador County, California (one of Eugene Hilgard's experimental vineyards; these selections became FPMS 09 and 16) and two (FPMS 13 and 15) from the same Martini vineyard from which Richard Sommer obtained his Pinot noir. Coury offered FPMS 13 in his nursery; however, it was never widely planted in Oregon. Erath offered the two from Amador County, and a number of growers planted these.

Meanwhile, the number of Willamette viniculturalists continued to grow. Dick Ponzi, another amateur winemaker from California, had met Coury during a 1969 visit to Forest Grove (home of Nancy Ponzi's parents) and decided that Oregon would be a good place to start a winery. He took a teaching position with Portland Community College and not long after that was visited by a textbook salesman named David Lett. Ponzi acquired property west of Tigard in 1970 and produced his first vintage in 1974.

Bill Fuller had been a classmate of Coury's and Lett's at UC Davis. After finishing school, he worked for Louis Martini for several years. In 1971, he partnered with San Francisco banker Bill Malkmus to start a winery and began looking at locations ranging from California's Anderson Valley to eastern Washington State. He finally acquired property in Oregon's Washington County about four miles north of Coury's and registered Tualatin Valley Vineyards in 1973. His first vintage was from that same year; it was, however, made from grapes grown in Washington State.

Bill Blosser and Susan Sokol Blosser arrived in Oregon in early 1970. Bill Blosser had just received a master's degree in city and regional planning at a university in North Carolina and had acquired a position with Portland State University. During the drive to Oregon, Bill broached the subject of starting a vineyard. After some discussion, they decided to move forward with the idea, purchasing property in December and planting vines over the winter. They sold the grapes from their first harvests to Lett and Erath, finally completing a winery in 1977. As the Blossers had no background in making wine, they hired Bob McRitchie, a winemaker from California. Sokol Blosser opened Oregon's first tasting room in 1978.

Myron Redford was a young winemaker from Seattle who was visiting Oregon in 1972. At the suggestion of a family friend, he visited Jerry and Ann Preston, owners of a small vineyard near Amity. In 1973, personal

Myron Redford and then partner Janis Checchia, 1974. *OWHA collection, donation of Amity Vineyards and Myron Redford.*

difficulties prompted Jerry Preston to abandon his plans for a winery, and in 1974 Redford purchased Preston's vineyard. Arriving in April, Redford found the vineyard to be suffering from neglect, with most of the vines dead. He ordered new vines from Charles Coury and planted them when they arrived in June. This was too late in the year, and half of these died. Redford persisted, mastering the agricultural side of the enterprise, building a winery and producing his first vintage in 1976.

David and Ginny Adelsheim were Portlanders who'd developed an appreciation for wine while visiting Europe in 1969. They decided they'd like to get into the business and, after learning that a friend worked for Bill Blosser, met with him at his office at Portland State University. The meeting went well, and Blosser invited them to a party at his home, where they met David and Diana Lett. Encouraged by all this, the Adelsheims started looking for property in Yamhill County. One day in early 1971, while driving around near Dundee, they spotted "a big bearded guy standing out in front of his house" and stopped to ask him if he knew of any wine grape vineyards in the area. The big bearded guy was Dick Erath, and he did.[189] The Adelsheims purchased property in June and built a house on it, planting vines the following year. Unfortunately, they planted too late in the year, and the vines did not do well. Realizing that he needed to improve his vinicultural knowledge, Adelsheim interned first with David Lett (in 1973) and then with Lycée Agricole et Viticole in Burgundy (1974). Returning to Oregon, in 1975 he hired two workers to help him with the vineyard and took a job to help cover the expense. Fortuitously, the position was as sommelier at Horst Mager's L'Omelette, a Portland restaurant favored by James Beard and Julia Child. Adelsheim added an Oregon section to the wine list, and Portland began to discover that some very fine wine was being made in its own backyard.

While David Adelsheim was in Burgundy, he made an interesting discovery; there, the Chardonnay and Pinot noir ripened at the same time, whereas Chardonnay in Oregon was ripening two weeks after Pinot noir. The Chardonnay clone Lett was growing (FPMS 05) might do well in California but often did not ripen in Oregon.

The growers, unhappy with the current selections available from FPMS and frustrated with that organization's disinterest in obtaining new clones, approached OSU about establishing its own vine importation program. (There was also the matter of the FPMS misidentification of "Gamay Beaujolais.") Dr. Ronald Cameron, an OSU plant pathologist, applied to the USDA for a permit to import, quarantine and distribute vines. The request was granted and the permit issued in 1975. With the assistance of Charles Coury, the university in 1976 obtained examples of Pinot blanc, Pinot gris, Gewürztraminer, Chasselas rouge and Sylvaner. (This last is a white grape grown in Alsace and in Germany.) These were received from INRA (Institut National de la Recherche Agronomique; National Institute of Agricultural Research) in Colmar, France, and were made available to growers in 1977 after a year of testing.[190] Only the first three varieties found many takers, and apparently only Charles Coury acquired any of the Sylvaner. As far as the author knows, no Chasselas rouge is commercially grown in Oregon.

OSU also received clones from French researcher Claude Valat of the IFV (Association Nationale Technique pour l'Amélioration de la Viticulture; Institute of Vine and Wine) in L'Espiguette, France. David Adelsheim had visited Valat and requested Pinot noir, Chardonnay and Gamay noir, and OSU subsequently received three selections of Pinot noir, two of Chardonnay and four of Gamay noir. One of each variety tested positive for viral infection. The two uninfected Pinot noir clones were numbered 236 (many years later becoming FPS 40) and 374 (FPS 100). The uninfected Chardonnay was clone 352 and was planted by a number of growers; according to David Adelsheim, it does well in sparkling wines. As for the Gamay noir, despite Lett and Coury's early plantings of "Gamay Beaujolais," by the mid-1970s there was not a lot of interest in this grape in Oregon. This second set of clones was released in 1978.[191]

OSU had not been idle during the period between the stillborn propagation project of 1970 and the importation program of 1975. One of the problems encountered by local vintners was the high acidity of the grapes; with many varietal wines a secondary fermentation, known as malolactic fermentation, is beneficial. Pinot noir is one such variety, but most being made in Oregon during this period were not achieving this and high acidity was believed to be the culprit. Hoya Yang, who had acquired in 1972 a license from the BATF for an experimental wine cellar, focused on finding a yeast that would reduce acidity (along with its usual role of converting sugar to alcohol). He obtained a strain known as Schizosaccharomyces pombe from a German enologist; this had the desired effect, and Yang made the yeast available to Oregon winemakers in 1974.[192]

The university also planted twenty varieties of *vinifera* vines in various locations around the state to see how they performed and shared the results with the winery owners.

OSU added Barney Watson to its team in 1976. A 1971 graduate from UC Davis, Watson was to provide invaluable assistance to the growers in the coming years. The year 1977 saw the retirement of Hoya Yang; with his departure, OSU lost its license to make wine.

The university also contributed in an indirect way with its development of "bush" beans; unlike "pole" beans, these could be harvested by machine and were quickly adopted by Oregon farmers. The result was a surplus of poles and wire, and the grape growers could obtain these for little or no cost, considerably reducing the expense of trellising their vines.[193]

Concurrent with the effort to obtain better selections of grapes, the growers were engaged in a proactive project to protect potential vineyard land. Oregon Senate Bill 100 was signed into law on May 29, 1973, and required counties to develop comprehensive land use plans for guiding zoning decisions. Much of the impetus for this law had come from the agricultural community, which was concerned about urban and suburban encroachment on agricultural lands. Bill Blosser was working for a company contracted to develop a land use plan for Portland and understood the implications for future vineyard development. According to Blosser:

> Soon after SB100 passed, I got involved in helping the county preserve prime vineyard lands. Dave Adelsheim was also very interested, so we teamed up.

I became a member of the local planning advisory committee working with the county on defining lands to be preserved (and shortly thereafter I went on the County Planning Commission). Dave led the process of creating the mapping criteria that we used to objectively define "prime" vineyard lands. We used these criteria to map all the prime vineyard lands in the Willamette Valley, and gave these maps and criteria to the counties around the valley. The same criteria were used in other parts of the state, with modifications to fit local conditions. Virtually all the counties used our criteria with little modification and adopted them into their plans, which is the reason so much vineyard land was designated "Prime Farm Land" in the state. We were very lucky to be there at the intersection of a time when the young wine industry was looking for ways to preserve prime vineyard sites and the counties were looking for criteria to use for their plans.[194]

David McDonald, Yamhill County's director of planning, welcomed the growers' input. The planning staff had solicited the community for criteria to guide the process and received little response up to this point. The growers were well organized and were offering clearly defined criteria and supporting documentation. Bill Blosser's expertise in land use planning was "critical" (David Adelsheim's word) to the success of the effort, and the growers found an ally in McDonald and his successor, Craig Greenleaf. Ultimately, the growers were successful; nearly all of the land the growers had shaded on their USGS maps remained zoned agricultural.

The three growers in Washington County (Coury, Fuller and Ponzi) did not make a similar effort; the feeling was that they were too few in number to succeed.[195] According to Blosser, "In Washington County there was a huge force behind developing the hillsides for homes," and there was, as a result, a great deal of political resistance to designating hillsides for vineyards.[196]

The next issue tackled by the growers was that of labeling. In a 2010 interview, Myron Redford stated that this originated as a reaction to Bill Fuller's use of the statement "Produced and Bottled by Tualatin Vineyards, Forest Grove, Oregon" on a bottle of wine made from Washington State grapes. This label could create the impression that the wine was an all-Oregon product, which it was not. Fuller defended his action by pointing to a BATF requirement that when grapes crossed a state line to be turned into wine, the wine label could not carry any place-of-origin appellation other than "American." (Another peculiarity of the rule was that a vintage date could not be used.) Fuller did not want to use the "American" appellation and used the "Produced and Bottled by" statement because he wanted the consumer to know it was from the Pacific Northwest.

In fact, most of the proposed labeling rules ultimately submitted to the OLCC (Oregon Liquor Control Commission) had nothing to do with Fuller's action; many reflected French criticism of California wines that carried French place names such as "Burgundy" or "Chablis." A number of the growers had visited France where producers and researchers had undoubtedly expressed their feelings on the subject. Frank Prial, a syndicated wine columnist with the *New York Times*, published on July 21, 1976, an article titled "American Wine Labelling Is a Disgrace, Reforms Are Necessary." In this article, Prial criticized both the use of European place names and the BATF's requirement that a varietal labeled wine need contain only 51 percent of the reference grape and pointed out loopholes in place-of-origin statements. He also reported that California wineries were trying to further weaken the regulations.

Prial's column was widely syndicated, and it's hard to believe that it wasn't read by some (if not all) of the Oregon growers and vintners. The column appeared after the growers had formulated their proposed rules, during the period when David Adelsheim was working on getting winemakers around the state to agree to them. (The OLCC required the winemakers to unanimously agree to the proposed rules before they could be adopted.) It's not a stretch to believe the Prial column helped convince Oregon winemakers that the new labeling rules would benefit the industry. One dissenter was Paul Bjelland, who'd started a winery in Douglas County in 1969. After it was agreed that his "Johannisberg Riesling" could be grandfathered in, he joined the other winemakers in supporting the proposed rules, which were finally adopted by the OLCC in 1977.

The new rules banned the use of European place names, required varietal labeled wines to be 90 percent composed of the reference grape (seven Bordeaux varieties were set to the lower standard of 75 percent) and required an appellation labeled bottle to be 100 percent composed of grapes from within the reference appellation. Limits were placed on the amount of sugar that could be added during fermentation (chaptalization), and diluting the wine with water was banned. The new rules were codified as an Oregon Administrative Rule (various sections of OAR 845-010) in 1977 and are still in effect today. (Some minor changes were made in 2007.)

As for the peculiar federal rule regarding wines made from out-of-state grapes, Dick Ponzi sent a letter (dated February 23, 1978) to Oregon congressman Les AuCoin; the letter described the rule and requested

AuCoin's assistance in getting it changed. The effort was successful; commencing with the 1978 vintage, a label could show the percentage of in-state and out-of-state grapes and bear a vintage date. (For example, an Amity label from the 1978 vintage bears the statement "57% Oregon–43% Washington.")[197]

The year 1977 also saw the creation of the Table Wine Research Advisory Board (WAB for short), an organization created to fund research efforts. The winegrowers voted to tax themselves at a rate of twelve dollars per ton of harvested grapes to fund the organization; again, the OLCC required unanimity among the growers as a prerequisite to its approval. The WAB funded Barney Watson's position at OSU for the next several years.

The winegrowers formed a series of associations during the 1969 to 1978 period. In the Willamette, Lett, Coury and Erath formed an ad hoc group known as the Oregon Viticultural Development Committee. In southern Oregon, Richard Sommer and Paul Bjelland formed the Umpqua Grape Growers Association in January 1969; Ted Maffitt (Humbug Winery) and vineyard owner Ted Anderson were members as well. The organization was short-lived, replaced by the Oregon Winegrowers Association (OWGA) in March; the membership expanded to include seven additional vineyard owners. Hoya Yang of OSU gave a presentation at one of the first meetings.

The Willamette growers soon joined as well, but quickly discovered that the Bjelland-led group was mostly a social gathering, lacking the technical content they wanted. In 1972, the Willamette winegrowers formed their own group, the Winegrowers Council of Oregon (WCO), gathering monthly in the meeting room of the Tigard fire station. These meetings were technical in nature, with the growers and winemakers sharing the knowledge they'd acquired from experience, classes and visits to France. It was also in these meetings that the winegrowers discussed the land use and labeling issues and decided on their course of action. Wine and cheese were served, but the wine was usually a California jug wine because the winemakers needed to sell all the wine they made.

The open information exchange that occurred in these meetings was a facet of the cooperation and coordination that existed among the Willamette winegrowers. They understood that they needed all the help they could get and that their peers were the best source for it. In interviews conducted by Linfield College during the early twenty-first century, the surviving members of the group all speak of the camaraderie that existed and cite examples of how the winegrowers assisted one another. Even David Lett

Susan Sokol Blosser in the Sokol
Blosser tasting room, 1979.
*OWHA collection, donation of Sokol
Blosser Winery and Susan Sokol Blosser.*

and Charles Coury, who'd fallen out during the late 1960s, remained civil
and cooperative with each other within the context of the group.

The Willamette group's first marketing effort came in 1978, when a
subset of the members published a brochure titled *Discovering Oregon Wine*.
This listed the five wineries that had regular tasting room hours and
included a map showing their locations. The brochure was designed by
commercial artist and vineyard owner Jack Myers, who also obtained
donated materials, which reduced the brochure's production cost.[198]

There were a number in the group who wanted the WAB replaced with
something that was still supported with taxes but included marketing in its
charter. There were legislators sympathetic to this, but they did not want
to contend with two competing industry groups. In 1978, the OWGA and
the WCO agreed to merge; there were a lot of details to work out, and
articles of confederation were not filed until 1981.

In 1979, Oregon wine salesman Stephen Cary decided to try extending
the Yamhill winegrowers' culture of information exchange and cooperation
to a wider group. The following year, he and a California winemaker
organized a small conference at the Steamboat Lodge on the Umpqua River.
Seventeen Pinot producers from Oregon and California attended; all were
encouraged to bring samples of their wines, both good and bad. The wines
were tasted blind and critiqued, with discussion centering on how they could
be improved. Comments were both frank and confidential; the conference
credo was (and still is), "What's said at Steamboat, stays at Steamboat."

On July 1, 1979, the IRS published its yearly list of bonded wineries. Thirty-one were listed for Oregon; of these, seventeen were making wine exclusively from grapes, and seven of these were within thirteen miles of Dundee. These were The Eyrie, Knudsen-Erath (in 1975, Dick Erath partnered with vineyard owner Cal Knudsen), Ponzi, Amity, Sokol Blosser, Adelsheim and Elk Cove (started by Joe and Pat Campbell; Pat was the great-granddaughter of Jacob Jungen, the Washington County winemaker mentioned in chapter 4). There were four exclusively grape wineries in Douglas County; these were HillCrest, Jonicole (started by three partners in 1975), Humbug Winery and Henry's Winery (Scott Henry, 1978). Central Washington County was the site of three more, these being Wine Hall Vineyards (Coury's former operation), Tualatin Vineyards and Cotes des Colombe (started in 1977 by Joe Colombe, a co-worker of Dick Erath's at Tektronix). Three additional all-grape wineries were Forgeron Vineyards in Elmira (first in the southern Willamette Valley), Siskiyou Vineyards in Cave Junction and in Jackson County's Applegate Valley, Frank Wisnovsky borrowed the name Valley View from Peter Britt's nineteenth-century winery. (**MYTH NUMBER NINE** asserts that the new Valley View was at the same location as the old one; in fact, the two vineyard locations are many miles apart.)

There were five wineries producing both grape and fruit wines. Four were in the Willamette Valley; Honeywood resumed making grape wine in 1978, Oak Knoll (near Hillsboro) was started in 1970 by Rob and Marjorie Vuylsteke, Century Home Wine (Newburg) was a small winery opened by Dave and Peggy Maze and Arterberry Winery (McMinnville) was founded in 1979 by Fred Arterberry. Arterberry had received a degree in fermentation sciences from UC Davis and was making *vinifera* wine as well as a sparkling hard apple cider. For his wine, he was purchasing grapes from Jim Maresh, who started a vineyard in 1970 at the suggestion of Dick Erath.

In Douglas County, Paul Bjelland was making wine from grapes and berries.

There were seven wineries making exclusively fruit wine, plus Honey House Winery in Veneta, which was making mead. There was also Shallon Winery in Astoria, which was adding fruit flavors to a whey wine base. Whey is a byproduct of cheese production, and during the mid-1970s, Hoya Yang of OSU developed a process for fermenting it (a neat trick, since whey is mostly protein). It was hoped whey wine would become a major product, but only a handful of small companies ever did anything with it.

There were also numerous independent vineyards around the state that sold grapes to wineries whose production capacity could not be filled with grapes from the winery's own vineyards (a pattern that continues to this day). In the autumn of 1976, there were three different vineyards advertising wine grapes in the classifieds of mid-valley newspapers.

THE GENESIS OF THE Oregon Pinot noir phenomenon cannot be attributed to a single individual or be said to have taken place at a single point in space and time. It was achieved over the course of the 1970s by a small number of viniculturalists working in the northern Willamette Valley. They were a diverse group, with a short list of traits all shared. They were intelligent and educated; all had at least a bachelor's degree and some a postgraduate degree. There were all lovers of Pinot noir, and all believed that the Willamette Valley was the ideal place to grow it. They were resourceful and determined to succeed; with a single exception, all who'd accepted the challenge were still in business at the end of the 1970s. With a single exception, none of them had ever grown grapes or made wine on a commercial scale, and with a single exception, all were operating with limited budgets. Nevertheless, they learned how to grow the vines, how to make the wine and how to sell it.

Some of them wanted to build an industry. Others had more limited goals; they wanted only to make the best wine they could and provide themselves and their families with a lifestyle consistent with their values. But even this latter group supported the goals of the first, and the initiatives of the 1970s created a foundation upon which an industry could be built. The acquisition of new clones of Pinot noir and other varieties, the successful effort to preserve the agricultural status of potential vineyard sites, the labeling laws that set a standard unmatched within the United States, the self-imposed tax to fund research and the organizations devoted to sharing hard-won knowledge all created an environment that nurtured the infant industry and paved the road for those who followed.

When The Eyrie 1975 South Block Reserve showed so brilliantly in Paris in 1979 and went on to do even better the following year in Burgundy, the wine world's gaze fell on Oregon. The Willamette winemakers did not shrink from that scrutiny; they welcomed it.

12

THE OREGONIAN, PART I

Jack Parker Myers was born in Corvallis on January 25, 1924. His parents divorced when he was quite young; the 1930 Census finds him living on his grandparent's farm near Corvallis. By 1940, he was living with his mother, an office clerk, in Oswego.

He grew tall (six feet, one inch) and was working as a logger when he enlisted in the army in 1942. He served in North Africa and Italy; after the war, he returned to Oregon, where he married Merle Idell "Miki" Volk in Portland on June 2, 1946. They both had an interest in art and attended Pratt Art School in Brooklyn over the next two years, after which they returned to Portland and started a commercial art company. He also taught graphic arts at Portland State. Jack and Miki had two sons and two daughters and moved to Aurora in 1967.

Jack loved wine and followed local newspapers' articles about the new wineries cropping up on the other side of the river. His first involvement came with a contract to design the label for Amity Vineyards. The contract was signed while Jerry Preston was the owner, but when Myron Redford acquired the property he liked the label enough to use it. Jack Myers also designed the first label for Erath.[199]

In 1974, he decided to start a vineyard. The property upslope of Amity Vineyards was for sale, and he borrowed Myron Redford's Cat D2 to look at it. (The Caterpillar D2 was a small tractor manufactured from 1938 to 1957, favored by vineyard owners because it was narrow enough to move between rows of vines and its tracks made it more mobile than a wheeled tractor.) While driving around the property, he hit a large rock; the impact threw him forward off the vehicle, knocking the wind out of him. When he regained consciousness, he saw that the tractor had stalled inches from his head. Returning to Redford's residence, he requested a "stiff drink."[200] He decided against the property next to Amity, which later became Bois Joli vineyard.

Driving to Yamhill County from Aurora would have taken him past the butte east of Champoeg, and he eventually inquired about buying the hillside property. The owner was willing to sell, and Jack acquired the property in mid-1974. The slope was covered with young Douglas-fir, and Jack hired a crew to help him clear it. As they approached the hill's crest, he found it.

The vine.

It was an ancient thing, thick and gnarled, its arms entwined around and up the nearest trees. Jack was mystified by its presence and equally mystified by the odd powdery finish on its leaves. He thought it might be diseased and wondered if it might pose a threat to his future vines, so he took samples to OSU. Even though this was long before DNA fingerprinting, it was easy enough to identify. It was Pinot Meunier; the leaves were *supposed* to look like that.

He didn't want the vine among those he'd planned for that part of the vineyard, but felt an obligation to preserve it. Before tearing it out, he took cuttings and was able to start new vines, which he planted on either side of the driveway into the vineyard. In the vineyard itself, he planted Pinot noir, Chardonnay, Pinot gris and Riesling.

His vineyard was successful, with sales to many of the Yamhill winemakers. He was a regular attendee to the winegrowers' meetings, where he was well liked. "He was incredible," recalled Myron Redford. "A great guy." He started a vineyard design and management business and in 1992 put in a vineyard for Cliff Anderson, who became a lifelong friend.

One year, a portion of his Pinot noir was missed during harvest. Discovering the overripe grapes, Jack called Dick Erath for advice. Erath happened to have some grape brandy on hand and suggested the grapes could be made into a port-style dessert wine, using the brandy to fortify the wine. It seemed like as good a plan as any, so the two made some port at Erath's winery.

During the late 1980s, he and Miki divorced, and she acquired half the vineyard. Jack wanted to buy it from her and partnered with an Arizona couple, William and Elise Pitterle, who had the capital to do it. The Pitterles wanted to start a winery, and construction started in 1992. The driveway into the property had to be widened, and this meant the Pinot Meunier vines would have to go. Again, Jack took cuttings and started new vines, with two planted at either end of the deck outside the winery's tasting room. The winery was completed in 1993.

Jack Myers parted with his share of the vineyard and winery not long after this. It's been said that the Pitterles took advantage of him to gain control of the property, but he turned seventy in 1994 and it may simply be that he was ready to retire and accepted less than market value for his share.

It was not long after this that the Pitterles abandoned the winery and returned to Arizona. The two Pinot Meunier vines began to take over the deck railings.

Jack retired to Aurora but remained friends with many of the growers and winemakers with whom he'd worked.

13

SECOND WAVE

1980–1998

After 1980 things really started happening in this valley.
—David Lett

Oregon's competitive success of 1980 was followed in 1984 when two wines, a 1980 Pinot noir and a 1981 Chardonnay from Tualatin Vineyards, took "Best of Show" at a competition in London. Money man Bill Malkmus made the trip to England to receive the awards from Queen Elizabeth; winemaker Bill Fuller was told to stay home and supervise the harvest.

In September 1985, a Burgundy-versus-Oregon blind tasting was held in New York. Conceived by Stephen Cary (then winemaker at Yamhill Valley Vineyards) and International Wine Center president Al Hotchkin, the event pitted ten Oregon Pinot noir wines against seven from Burgundy; all the wines were from the 1983 vintage. The Pinot from Yamhill Valley Vineyards took first place, with one from Sokol Blosser taking second and one from Adelsheim taking third. A Pinot from The Eyrie tied with a Burgundy for fourth, and Knudsen-Erath tied with another Burgundy for fifth. The judges, all experienced Burgundy drinkers, could not reliably tell the Oregon wines from the Burgundies. The results were reported in the *New York Times* and *Wine Spectator* (albeit on page 6).

Critics contended the Burgundies were too young. The competition was repeated in 1987, with the same wines and the same judges. Again, the Oregon wines dominated, taking six of the top seven places. A Pinot from The Eyrie tied for first place with one from Sokol Blosser.

Elements of the media had also discovered Oregon wine. In 1981, the *New York Times* published a profile of Ponzi Vineyards, and Frank Prial wrote a favorable review of the Ponzi 1979 Pinot noir. This was followed, on November 4, by an article from Harvey Steinman, wine critic for the *San Francisco Examiner*. Steinman reported the results of a tasting organized by him and two writers for *Vintage* magazine, Hank Rubin and Norm Roby. The trio tasted 174 Pinots from California, Oregon and Washington, all from the 1978, 1979 and 1980 vintages. The top two wines were the 1979 Ponzi and a 1979 Acacia. (This latter wine was made from grapes grown in California's cool Carneros Hills district.) Of the Ponzi, Steinman wrote, "The Ponzi…had a perfume-y, cherry-strawberry fragrance, good balance, and a long finish. It was everything one could want in a Pinot noir—and at $8, about half the price of the Acacia." Steinman also liked three wines from Knudsen-Erath (the 1978 and 1979 Vintage Select and the 1979 Yamhill County), the 1978 Tualatin Valley Vineyards, the 1979 Amity and a non-vintage bottling from Elk Cove. "The Oregon wines, almost without exception, had that appealing lightness of body, and the best examples had rich flavors as well."

In 1984, Portland wine store owner Rachel Starr sent a selection of Oregon wines to wine critic Robert Parker. Parker was impressed and traveled to Oregon to visit the state's wineries and sample more wines. In a letter to Myron Redford of Amity, dated September 11, 1985, he writes:

> *I should say that I have never written a letter like this before, but I must admit that I was quite astonished by the consistent high quality of [Oregon's] pinot noirs and chardonnays. First, they exhibited balance and unadulterated purity of fruit, with an underlying complexity that seems to swell and improve in the glass as the wine sits.*

> *I am especially impressed that each of you have given your wines a personal, individualistic style rather than trying to imitate each other. Congratulations!—I think what you have accomplished in 1983 with pinot noir is the most exciting development in the domestic wine industry in more than a decade.*[201]

Parker went on to write an enthusiastic article about Oregon in the October edition of his newsletter, the *Wine Advocate*, and followed this with articles in *Connoisseur* magazine and the *Washington Post*.

The two back-to-back events of 1985 (the New York tasting in September and Parker's newsletter in October) triggered an upsurge of interest in

Oregon wine. Susan Sokol Blosser reports their winery had, at the beginning of September, in inventory an estimated two-year supply; instead, this sold out in two months.[202]

Sale of Oregon wines was facilitated by Cary Oregon Wines, a brokerage company founded in 1983 by Stephen Cary and partner Reuben Rich. The company sold Oregon wine to distributors from California to New York.

In 1981, the merger of the OWGA and the WCO was finalized; the new organization was known as the Oregon Winegrowers Association (OWA). The organization was divided into four regional groups, these being the North Willamette, the South Willamette, the Umpqua and the Rogue. Each had three members on the OWA board; there were three additional board members elected statewide.

One of the first products of the new association was the *Oregon Winegrape Grower's Guide*, a compilation of the knowledge accumulated over the previous fifteen years. A foreword by Peter Lombard of the OSU Department of Horticulture was followed by eleven articles, including "Site and Varietal Selection" (David Lett), "Vineyard Layout and Site Preparation" (consultant Joel Myers, working at The Eyrie), "Spacing, Training and Trellising" (David Adelsheim, with diagrams by Jack Myers), "Practical Vineyard Management" (Susan Sokol Blosser) and "Vineyard Economics" (Terry Casteel and Jack Trenhaile). The first edition was published in 1983.

The increased membership of the OWA generated more dues revenue and allowed it to hire a lobbyist; consultant Bill Nelson, who'd been working for both the OWGA and the WCO, was tapped for this role.

With the state's growers and vintners united in a single organization, the Oregon legislature was willing to replace the Table Wine Research Advisory Board with a new organization, the Oregon Wine Advisory Board (OWAB). Funded by an increased wine grape tax (twenty-five dollars/ton) and operating under the auspices of the Oregon Department of Agriculture, the OWAB funded both research and marketing efforts. The enabling legislation was signed into law in 1983.

Having increased funds for research, OSU was able to fund a full-time professor of enology, and David Heatherbell of New Zealand was hired for the position. Heatherbell chose the scenic route to Oregon, which took him through France, where he met Raymond Bernard at INRA in Colmar. Heatherbell took the opportunity to request additional Pinot noir and Chardonnay clones, and the French, who were feeling quite friendly toward Oregon thanks to the state's labeling rules, were happy to accommodate. OSU soon received five new Pinot noir clones (113, 114, 115, 667 and 777)

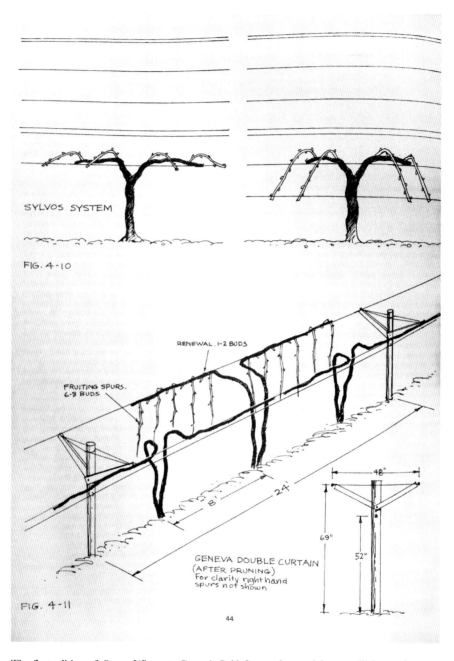

SYLVOS SYSTEM

FIG. 4-10

RENEWAL, 1-2 BUDS

FRUITING SPURS,
6-8 BUDS

8'

24'

48"

69"

52"

GENEVA DOUBLE CURTAIN
(AFTER PRUNING)
For clarity right hand
spurs not shown

FIG. 4-11

44

The first edition of *Oregon Winegrape Grower's Guide* featured an article on trellising and training systems, authored by David Adelsheim and illustrated by Jack Myers. *Photo by the author; permission to use granted by the Oregon Winegrowers Association and Ted Casteel.*

Oregon governor Victor Atiyeh signs the legislation that creates the OWAB, 1983. *From left to right*: Myron Redford, Bill Nelson, Scott Henry, State Senator Tony Meeken, Dick Erath, Governor Atiyeh, Ben Mafit, Richard Sommer, Marjorie Vuylsteke, Ronald Vuylsteke of Oak Knoll Winery and an unidentified but happy to be there woman. *OWHA collection, donation of Dick Erath.*

and four Chardonnay (75, 76, 96 and 98; Note: these are French numbers, not FPMS). A visit by David Adelsheim in 1988 resulted in three more Chardonnay clones (77, 95 and 277).

These new clones were all shipped from Dijon and became known as the "Dijon Clones," a name that often creates the impression they are all similar, which they definitely are not. The most popular of the Pinot noir clones (at least in Oregon) is 115, a consistent grape that strikes a middle ground in aromas, flavors and tannin. Clone 777 is something of an anomaly for Pinot noir, being deeply colored and tannic, with aromas and flavors of black cherry, cassis, leather and tobacco. Usually blended with wine from other clones to add color and depth, there are some all-777 bottlings. The author recently included one (the 2013 ArborBrook 777 Block) as a "ringer" in a tasting of Grenache-Syrah-Mourvèdre blends; none of the participants (all experienced wine drinkers) ever suspected it was Pinot noir.

OSU, in addition to importing, testing and distributing new grape clones, continued to work on the malolactic fermentation problem. The pombe yeast made available by Hoya Yang in 1974 turned out to be a less-than-satisfactory solution; unless sulphur was added to the fermenting wine, wild yeasts would overwhelm the pombe. Both David Lett and Dick Erath had produced some wine that had managed to undergo malolactic fermentation, and in the mid-1980s, OSU enologists took samples of these for analysis. Two different strains of bacteria were isolated in the two different wines; both could induce malolactic fermentation in high-acid wines. Cultures of the two strains were combined and commercially licensed by OSU.

By the mid-1980s, the Oregon-Burgundy connection, which originated with Oregon winegrowers visiting France to see how it was done there, was bringing Burgundians to Oregon for the same reason. One such was Véronique Drouhin, daughter of Robert Drouhin, the individual who'd organized the 1980 competition in which

Robert Drouhin, founder of Domaine Drouhin Oregon, attending the International Pinot Noir Celebration. *OWHA collection, donation of the IPNC.*

The Eyrie South Block Reserve had created such a sensation. Véronique spent time as an intern at Adelsheim, Bethel Heights and The Eyrie, but she also had a (semi) secret mission: she was scouting potential vineyard property for her father.

In 1987, Robert Drouhin announced the purchase of one hundred acres just southwest of Dundee; in February 1988, he purchased forty more. The new winery would be known as Domaine Drouhin Oregon, and Véronique (who'd received a degree in enology from the University of Dijon in 1986) would be its winemaker. Completed in 1989 in time for that year's vintage, DDO has been producing fine Pinot noir and Chardonnay ever since. (The author is particularly fond of their Chardonnay.)

In an article published on July 6, 1988 ("Pinot Noir Finds a New Home in Oregon Vineyards"), Frank Prial describes the Drouhin project and goes on to highlight the Oregon wine industry. "Oregon, many wine experts agree," wrote Prial, "consistently produces the finest pinot noir in the United States."

And there it was.

In December 1983, Oregon received its first American Viticultural Area (AVA), this being for the Willamette Valley.[203] An AVA is a designated wine-growing area, one which the winery can put on its label. AVAs were relatively new; the first had been assigned to the area around the town of Augusta in Missouri in 1980 (yes, Missouri), with the second assigned to Napa Valley shortly thereafter. In 1984, Oregon received three more, these being the Umpqua Valley, the Columbia Valley and the Walla Walla Valley (these last two shared with Washington State).

Most of the wineries founded during the 1980s were located in the Willamette Valley AVA, and though several notable ones were in Yamhill County (such as Rex Hill, Cameron, Argyle and Panther Creek), even more were started elsewhere in the valley. These included Montinore (south of Forest Grove), Hinman (west of Eugene), Bethel Heights (west of Salem), Serendipity (southwest of Monmouth), Tyee (south of Corvallis), Broadley (Monroe), Arlie (next door to Serendipity), Evesham Wood (west of Salem), Willamette Valley Vineyards (south of Salem), Argyle (Dundee) and Eola Hills Wine Cellars (Rickreall).

Tyee was a joint venture between OSU viticultural specialist Barney Watson and farmer David Buchanan, whose family had owned the property since the 1880s. In an interview with Linfield College, Watson recalled that when he told Myron Redford about it, Redford's comment was, "Well, Barney, now you'll have to take your own damn advice."

Serendipity Cellars was notable for unusual varietal bottlings. In addition to Pinot noir, owner/producer Glen Longshore was producing Chenin blanc, Zinfandel, Müller-Thurgau and Maréchal Foch. Müller-Thurgau is a cross of Riesling with Madeleine Royale, a grape popular in Germany because it ripened even earlier than Chasselas, while Maréchal Foch is a *riparia x rupestris x vinifera* hybrid. How Maréchal Foch got to Oregon is something of a mystery. Viticulturalist Philip Wagner (mentioned in chapter 2 in reference to the "foxiness" of *Vitis labrusca*) reports having sent samples to several Oregon growers during the 1940s.[204] It might be from one of them that Longshore's neighbor Archie Meadows obtained vines, which he planted in 1971. (Dick Erath also planted some Foch at about the time, but mostly as an experiment). Sometime during the early 1980s, Longshore purchased enough Maréchal Foch from Meadows to make seventy-five cases of wine. Pleased with the result, Longshore encouraged other growers in the area to plant Foch, which he continued to bottle on its own and also added small amounts to Pinot noir to darken the color. (Regulations allowed the wine to include up to 5 percent Foch.) Montinore Estate winery also planted eight acres of Maréchal Foch for the same purpose.[205] How many Oregon Pinot producers also blended Foch with Pinot will probably never be known. It's unlikely anyone does this anymore; Pinot noir clone 777 can likewise be used to add color and depth, and its availability eliminated the need to use Foch for this purpose. Maréchal Foch continues to be bottled by a number of Oregon wineries. (Arlie took over Serendipity's Foch and Müller-Thurgau when Longshore retired in 2001.) Because Foch is a grape that improves as the vine ages, if you want to try it, look for "Old Vine" on the label.

Argyle was founded in 1987 by Texan Rollin Soles and Australian Brian Croser. Though the original plan was to produce only sparkling wine, in 1992 the winery began producing table wines as well.

Willamette Valley Vineyards was the creation of Jim Bernau. Raised in Roseburg, his father, Fred Bernau, was Richard Sommer's attorney and would frequently bring home bottles of HillCrest wine. Jim and older brother John were so impressed by Sommer's wine that at age ten and twelve, respectively, they started making wine at home, initially using supermarket grape juice and later buying grapes from area growers. Despite this early interest in wine, Jim Bernau appeared to be moving in a different direction, winning a scholarship from the Oregon Association of Realtors for having won a speech contest. (A photo in his high school yearbook shows him behind an imposing trophy.) After receiving a degree in political science, Bernau became a lobbyist for the National Federation of Independent Businesses. Richard Sommer and Scott Henry were both members of this organization and asked Bernau to assist with the OWA's effort to pass the legislation it wanted.[206] Bernau worked with Bill Nelson and legislative staffer Joe Olexa on the effort. Olexa was starting his own vineyard, Ankeny, and began planting in 1982. Varieties included Pinot noir, Pinot gris and Maréchal Foch. Working with all these winemakers inspired Bernau to start a winery, and he began looking for a site. His first criterion was suitability for a vineyard, with high visibility determining the final selection. In 1983, he purchased hilly property just east of Interstate 5 south of Salem; a winery on a hillside would be visible from the highway, and nearby interchanges both north and south provided easy access. Bernau began clearing the property and planting vines while researching ways to finance construction of a winery. He first considered what today would be called a crowd-funding approach, but legal obstacles prevented this option. Bernau took the unprecedented step of forming a public corporation, and his public stock offering attracted enough investors to complete the winery by 1989. By 1992, Willamette Valley Vineyards had the highest production of any Oregon winery.

Eola Hills Wine Cellars was founded by Tom Huggins, who purchased land west of Salem and planted it with Pinot noir and Chardonnay. The winery's first wine was produced in 1986.

Back in Yamhill County, nine winery owners formed the Yamhill County Wineries Association in 1983. The owners recognized that publicizing their mutual proximity would draw more visitors and published a guide and map showing the location of their wineries. The association members opened their wineries for "Thanksgiving Weekend in Wine Country," starting a tradition that has become almost universal in Oregon.

In 1989, the Willamette had 3,615 acres of wine grapevines. 42 percent was Pinot noir, 23 percent was Chardonnay, 14 percent was Riesling, 6 percent was Pinot gris, 5 percent was Gewürztraminer, with the remaining 10 percent made up of other varieties.[207] The three largest producing estate wineries (in Oregon, not just the Willamette) were Knudsen Erath, Sokol Blosser and Tualatin Valley. According to Frank Prial, in 1987 these three accounted for 75 percent of the state's production[208] (Note: the qualifier

The nine founders of the Yamhill County Wineries Association toast the inaugural "Thanksgiving Weekend in Wine Country" in 1983. *Standing, from left to right*: Bill Blosser, Don Byard (Hidden Springs Winery), Myron Redford, Dick Erath, Fred Arterberry, Fred Benoit (Chateau Benoit Winery) and David Lett; *kneeling, left to right*: Joe Campbell and David Adelsheim. *OWHA collection, donation of The Eyrie Vineyards and Jason Lett.*

"estate" is important; Honeywood was still the state's largest producer but owned no vineyards. The Salem winery had begun making *vinifera* wine in 1978, but most of its production was still fruit wine.)

In the Umpqua Valley, most of the wineries started during the 1980s did not survive the decade. One exception was Girardet, started by Swiss immigrant Philippe Girardet. As a young man, Girardet had made wine in Switzerland but found the rules too restrictive. He earned an engineering degree and immigrated to the United States, where he found a job as staff engineer for the California Institute of Technology. In 1969, at age forty, he married twenty-four-year-old Bonnie Wallace, a wine lover and self-described hippie. Vacationing in Oregon in 1970, they visited HillCrest and decided the Umpqua Valley would be a good place to put down roots, purchasing fifty-four acres and building a cabin. The following year, they took their VW van on a vine-buying road trip that ranged from California to the state of New York. They returned with a wide assortment of varieties; Cabernet Sauvignon, Pinot noir, Chardonnay, Riesling and, from New York, the hybrid varieties Baco noir, Seyval blanc and Cayuga. Baco noir, a dark-skinned *riparia x vinifera* grape, is generally considered one of the better hybrids for red wine. Seyval blanc is a *vinifera x rupestris x aestivalis* hybrid used for white wine, and Cayuga is a cross of Seyval blanc with another hybrid. With *Vitis aestivalis* in their ancestry, Seyval blanc and Cayuga both ripen very early, and Cayuga is an extremely high-yielding vine. All three of these hybrids are resistant to phylloxera and other pests.

For their first ten years, the Girardets sold their grapes, but they started building a winery in 1982. It was completed in 1984, and their wine production eventually increased to the point where they had to start buying grapes, notably from the Doerners, who'd been expanding their acreage for some time.

Scott Henry was doing well and experimenting with trellising systems to alleviate bunch rot. In 1982, he devised a successful system that is now widely used in Oregon, New Zealand and other areas where bunch rot is a problem.

Richard Sommer's HillCrest was also doing well, but the same could not be said for the Umpqua's second modern winemaker, Paul Bjelland. His wines were not popular (Philippe Girardet describes them as "atrocious"), and he sold his winery in 1989.

In 1989, there were 386 acres of wine grapes in Douglas County. 21 percent was Chardonnay, 20 percent was Pinot noir, 19 percent was Riesling,

17 percent was Cabernet Sauvignon, with Gewürztraminer, Sauvignon blanc and others accounting for the balance.[209]

In Jackson County, Frank Wisnovsky's Valley View was producing Cabernet Sauvignon, Merlot and Chardonnay. Located at the northern end of the Applegate Valley, the vineyard had been planted in 1972 and produced its first commercial-size harvest in 1976. Wisnovsky did not yet have a winery, so grapes from both the 1976 and 1977 harvests were shipped to Tualatin Valley Vineyards to be made into wine and bottled under the Valley View label. The Valley View winery, converted from an old barn, was ready in time for the 1978 vintage. Wisnovsky hired Guy Ruhland as winemaker; Ruhland's credentials included an enology degree from UC Davis and experience at Tualatin Valley and Knudsen-Erath. John Eagle was hired to do vineyard maintenance and to assist Ruhland. The 1978 Cabernet Sauvignon turned out well, and the 1979 was looking promising when Ruhland left after a dispute with Wisnovsky. Eagle was able to produce a good wine and was subsequently promoted to winemaker.[210]

In July 1980, Frank Wisnovsky was killed in a diving accident. Anna Wisnovsky was able to keep the enterprise going with help from John Eagle and former vineyard manager Lee Rickords, who returned after Wisnovsky's death.

Joe Ginet was the grandson of early twentieth-century viniculturalist Joseph Ginet. The family had lost their farm during the Great Depression, but with Valley View's success, Ginet hoped a bank would finance a vineyard and winery. Unfortunately, none would, but one loan officer suggested that a loan for a more conventional farm would probably be approved, so Ginet submitted a proposal for a dairy farm. He got the loan, purchased land and cows and spent the next twenty years operating a dairy farm. During the mid-1990s, he picked out a spot for a vineyard and began planting vines.

Out in Illinois Valley (location of Cave Junction), Siskiyou Vineyards was founded in 1978 by Charles and Susan David. The six-acre vineyard was planted with Pinot Noir, Cabernet Sauvignon and Gewürztraminer. Charles David died in 1983, but Susan and winemaker Donna Devine kept the operation going until 1997, when the vineyard was sold.

Another Illinois Valley winegrower was Ted Gerber, whose Foris Winery was bonded in 1981. Gerber's enterprise has been a successful one, growing from 15 acres of vines to 255 today.

Two wineries were started near Ashland, both bonded in late 1988. Ashland Vineyards and Winery was started by Philip Kodak and at once time boasted a 120-acre vineyard; recent reports suggest the operation is dying a slow death. More successful was Weisinger Family Winery, founded by John Weisinger, who'd been growing grapes since 1979. The winery is currently operated by son Eric Weisinger.

There were 411 acres of wine grapes growing in the Rogue Valley in 1989. 25 percent was Pinot noir, 24 percent Chardonnay, 19 percent was Cabernet Sauvignon, 9 percent Gewürztraminer, with other varieties comprising the remaining 23 percent.[211]

Along the Columbia River, but west of the Columbia Valley AVA, Cliff and Eileen Blanchette started Hood River Vineyards in 1981. They produced fruit wines from their orchards and grape wines from a twelve-acre vineyard. The winery is still operating today but has had new owners since 1993.

South of The Dalles, the old Mesplie farm was acquired in 1982 by Robert Foster, a cherry farmer. Foster hoped to resurrect the old Zinfandel vineyard and had hired six women to help him with the pruning. They met in the vineyard one morning to start work and were joined by Lonnie Wright, owner of a vineyard management company based in Hood River. Wright had heard of the project from his wife, who knew two of the women in Foster's crew. Wright offered to take on management of the vineyard,

The Pines Zinfandel vineyard south of The Dalles is the oldest vineyard of on-their-own-roots grapevines in Oregon. (There are isolated relic vines scattered around the state that may be older.) *Photo by the author.*

and Foster agreed, realizing that a professional would have a better chance of succeeding with the project. Wright and the crew (which lost half of its members the first day) pruned the seven acres of vines, after which Wright staked them and installed a drip irrigation system. Astonishingly, about 90 percent of the vines recovered. Several years later, Foster found himself unable to continue with payments on the property and turned it back over to the seller, Ken Melby, a Salt Lake City businessman. Melby asked Wright to continue managing the property; in exchange, Wright and his family could live on the farm, paying only nominal rent. At that point in time, Wright didn't know who'd originally put in the vineyard, but over the next several years, members of the Comini family came forward and told Wright about Luigi Comini and his winemaking.[212]

Bill Swain was another graduate of the UC Davis enology program. Visiting the Columbia Gorge in 1977, he decided it would be a good place to grow grapevines and purchased property for a vineyard in 1979. Swain's vineyard was on the Washington side of the river, but he put his winery in Hood River because of its transportation advantages. Three Rivers Winery operated from 1983 until 1994, when the Swains, who had three daughters, decided to move to an area with a better school system.

The 1989 Oregon Vineyard Report records 835 acres of wine grapevines on the Oregon side of the Columbia River. 29 percent was Riesling, 19 percent was Chardonnay, 10 percent was Pinot noir, 9 percent was Cabernet Sauvignon, 8 percent was Gewürztraminer, with other varieties accounting for 25 percent of the acreage.

THE PINOT NOIR WINEGROWERS conference (first held at Steamboat Lodge in 1980) met the following year in Napa Valley. The conference was less successful, because for reasons obscured by the haze of time, the California participants all left in time to be home by 4:20 p.m. In 1982, it was back at Steamboat. The year 1983 saw another attempt to hold it in Napa; again, the result was less than satisfactory. Since 1984, it has been held at the Steamboat Lodge.

Another annual event was inaugurated in 1987, the International Pinot Noir Celebration. Conceived by a number of McMinnville businesses (chiefly restaurants) and local wineries, the three-day event includes presentations and seminars but mostly consists of wining and dining. Wineries from all over the world are represented, all pouring samples of their Pinot noir. The event is held on the campus of Linfield College in late July.

Reporting the event was *Oregon Wine*, a monthly publication started by husband-and-wife team Richard Hopkins and Elaine Cohen in 1984. Originally titled *The Oregon Wine Calendar* and consisting of a few stapled pages, as advertising revenue grew, the publication became a more polished product. The magazine included a calendar of events, news articles and winery profiles. With the July 1987 issue (the first under the *Oregon Wine* name), a Restaurant of the Month feature was added, along with a directory of wineries. Hopkins also contributed editorials; a recurring theme was that the state and its wineries should do more to promote tourism.

One step in that direction was the appearance, in the late 1980s, of the ubiquitous blue signs showing the direction to nearby wineries. Bill Fuller of Tualatin Valley Vineyards had lobbied Congress to grant Oregon an exception allowing the state to put such signs on federally maintained highways. The Oregon legislature then had to be lobbied to take advantage of the exception.

THE 1990s OPENED WITH two unhappy events, the first being the death, at age thirty-seven, of Fred Arterberry. Arterberry, who'd produced Oregon's first sparkling wine, was on track to become one of the state's premier winemakers. He'd married Martha Maresh (daughter of vineyard owner Jim Maresh) in 1980, and in 1983 Martha gave birth to a son, James. With Arterberry's death, the winery closed.

The second event, far more ominous, was the discovery of phylloxera in a vineyard near Dundee. The pest has since been slowly spreading through the state's vineyards, forcing owners to tear out the old vines and replace them with vines grafted onto resistant rootstock. Many starting new vineyards in the area began using resistant rootstock with their initial plantings.

Despite the appearance of the pest, Oregon viniculture experienced a growth spurt from 1990 to 1992. The number of wineries, which had increased from seventy-one in 1988 to seventy-four in 1990, jumped to ninety-four by 1992. The state's success with Pinot noir was attracting more winemakers (both experienced and not) and more investors.

One such was wine critic Robert Parker, who formed a partnership with his wife's brother, Michael Etzel, to purchase a Yamhill County farm and convert it to viticulture. Etzel began planting Pinot noir in 1986 and, while waiting for the vines to mature, worked at Ponzi winery. Etzel's first harvest was in 1990, with most of his grapes sold to Ponzi and Panther

King Estate, west of Eugene, was founded in 1992. *Photo by the author.*

Creek. In 1991, the brothers-in-law recruited a third partner, Robert Roy, and converted a barn into a winery. Beaux Frères produced its first wine in 1992. Those familiar with Parker know that he favors highly extracted, oaky wines, and this preference was reflected in the wines for many years.

Edward King III purchased property west of Eugene in 1990 and founded King Estate two years later. A large and impressive winery complex was constructed atop a hill at the edge of the Oregon coast range, commanding a view of hundreds of acres of vines. King Estate focused on Pinot gris as its signature white wine, producing it in quantity and distributing it nationally. (The author's first Oregon Pinot gris was a King Estate, ordered off the wine list in a restaurant in St. Augustine, Florida.)

Other noteworthy wineries established in the Willamette Valley included Cristom (whose winemaker Steve Doerner was hired from Calera, one of the better California Pinot noir producers), Brick House, WillaKenzie (one of the first to plant all its vines on resistant rootstock), Chehalem, St. Innocent (which had produced its first wine in 1988 at Arterberry but didn't have its own premises until 1994) and Sineann.

Sineann, then located in Newberg, had no vineyards of its own. Partners Peter Rosback and David O'Reilly planned to produce wine from a number of varieties sourced from notable vineyards. Their first bottling, in 1994, was Old Vine Zinfandel from Lonnie Wright's vineyard south of The Dalles. Wright planned to acquire the vineyard as soon as he could and was concerned that someone might buy it out from under him. The Sineann label gave only "Columbia Valley" as the appellation, and many (probably most) people assumed it was from Washington State. It was tagged as such in the *Wine Advocate* review, which stated that it

> *tastes like it was made in the Russian River Valley. The wine possesses tons of black-raspberry and cherry fruit, a wonderfully expansive, chewy, multi-layered texture, and a voluptuously rich, spicy finish. It is fermented with wild yeast and aged in new French and American oak. Although extremely limited in availability, it is well-worth an effort to obtain a bottle or two.*[213]

By 1998, there were eighty-three wineries in the Willamette Valley; thirty-three were in Yamhill County. There were 6,722 acres of wine grapes in the valley. Of these, 50 percent was Pinot noir, 18 percent Chardonnay, 17 percent Pinot gris, 6 percent Riesling and other varieties accounting for the remaining 9 percent.[214] Pinot noir and Pinot gris were on the rise, Chardonnay and Riesling in decline.

In Umpqua Valley AVA, the most significant new winery was Abacela. Earl Jones was a medical researcher who made frequent trips to Europe, with Spain being his favorite destination. He liked the people, the food and the wine, and of the wines, he favored the Tempranillo-based wines of Rioja and the Ribera del Duero districts. Deciding that he wanted to make Tempranillo in the United States, he studied the climate of various viticultural areas in California and Oregon and settled on the Umpqua Valley. He purchased land in 1995, planted Tempranillo vines and produced his first wine in 1998. He entered the wine in the San Francisco International Wine Competition, where it won the Tempranillo category, besting all the Spanish entries. Abacela went on to add a number of warm-weather varieties, including Grenache, Malbec, Merlot, Syrah, Viognier and Albariño.

There were seven wineries in the Umpqua AVA in 1998 and 582 acres of wine grapes. Pinot noir accounted for 22 percent of the acreage, with Chardonnay taking 17 percent. The balance was spread across numerous other varieties, from Albariño (at Abacela) to Zinfandel. (The Doerners had Zinfandel vines dating back to the late 1880s.)

The Rogue Valley acquired its own AVA in 1991. By 1998, there were ten wineries in Jackson and Josephine Counties, with 1,009 acres of vines.

Merlot had the highest percentage, at 24 percent, with Pinot noir in second place at 17 percent. The most notable new winery of the 1990s was Troon. Richard Troon had started growing wine grapes during the 1970s (Cabernet Sauvignon and Zinfandel), and wines bearing the Troon name appeared with the 1993 vintage.

Along the Columbia, there were only five wineries in 1998 and 687 acres of vines.

BY THE 1990s, MANY of the wineries started in the '70s and '80s were financially secure, and a number of the owners felt it was time to give something back. In 1981, eighteen of them created the ¡Salud! Organization, the goal of which is to provide healthcare services to the migrant vineyard workers and their families. Funded by an annual wine auction (the first held in 1982), the program was inspired by a long-running (since 1859) auction in Burgundy, the proceeds from which are donated to the hospital in Beaune. In Oregon, the number of participating wineries has grown to over one hundred.

The social consciousness of many Oregon growers and winemakers also inspired environmental stewardship. From the beginning, most of them had followed viticultural methods that minimized the use of pesticides and chemical fertilizers. During the 1990s, efforts were made to formalize these practices. The first of these was Salmon-Safe, a program intended to maintain water purity in rivers and streams in the Pacific Northwest, started by the Pacific Rivers Council. Farms and vineyards that meet the organization's standards are certified as such. In 1996, Sokol Blosser was the first Oregon winery to receive the certification.

A more comprehensive certification is LIVE (Low Input Viticulture and Enology), which sets standards for sustainable farming practices. Carmo Vasconcelos, a viticultural researcher hired by OSU in 1994, had worked in Europe and was familiar with the "integrated production" approach promoted by the International Organization for Biological Control (IOBC). She found many Oregon winegrowers receptive to the concept and, working with Ted Casteel and other growers, created LIVE in 1997. The LIVE program was certified by the IOBC in 2001, the first such program certified in the United States.[215]

The mid-1990s also saw new legislation. Wineries were allowed to ship directly to buyers, which enabled the wine clubs now offered by most of the state's wineries. Other legislation permitted wine and grocery stores to hold in-store tastings, allowing customers to sample a wine before buying it.

Dick Erath in the Erath Winery barrel room, 1995. *OWHA collection, donation of Dick Erath.*

DURING THE 1993 TO 1998 period, there was only modest growth in the number of Oregon wineries, from 96 to 105. The vineyard acreage increase was more substantial, from 6,250 acres to 9,000. It was a maturation period for the industry, as grape growers and winemakers refined their techniques and Oregon wine continued to gain market share. Slow and steady growth characterized these six years.

All that was about to change.

LIFT OFF

S ince 1999, the Oregon wine industry has experienced phenomenal growth, with many hundreds of wineries operating by the middle of the twenty-first century's second decade. The exact number varies depending on the source; the United States Department of the Treasury, Alcohol and Tobacco Tax and Trade Bureau reports 602 bonded wineries in Oregon for 2015. The Oregon Vineyard and Winery Census Report, compiled by the Southern Oregon University Research Center, adds another 100 to that figure; the Census Report includes OLCC-issued winery licenses and "Growers Sales Privilege" (a license which, according to the OLCC, "Allows the importation, storage, transportation, export, & wholesale & retail sales of wines made from fruit or grapes grown in Oregon."").

The number is also inflated by "virtual wineries." A 1999 Oregon law permits multiple licensees to operate within a single premise, and many winemakers have taken advantage of this. The most notable example is the Carlton Winemakers Studio, which at any given time has a dozen or more winemakers using its facilities. Though not owning its own building, a "virtual winery" is still a distinct business entity, with its own winemaker and label. Including these brings the total number of Oregon wineries to over 800 by the end of 2018.

The number of physical wineries also numbers in the hundreds. The 2016 Census reports 424 "wineries crushing grapes." The number will certainly exceed 500 by 2020.

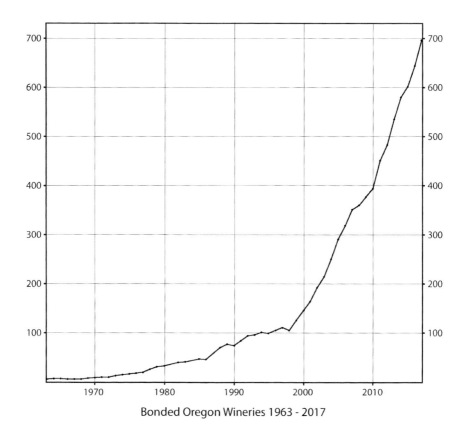

Bonded Oregon Wineries 1963 - 2017

Since 1999, the number of Oregon wineries has increased dramatically. *Graph by the author.*

The first generation of modern wineries had been around for thirty years or more, and changes were taking place at all of them. Richard Sommer sold HillCrest in 2003, and the new owner, Dyson DeMara, has made numerous changes. Some of these were forced; phylloxera has been spreading in the Umpqua Valley, and all of Sommer's original vines had to be pulled and replaced with vines on resistant rootstock. Pinot noir is still being made at HillCrest, of course, but Abacela's success with warm-climate varieties has encouraged DeMara to plant Tempranillo and Malbec. The new plantings of Sommer's favorite grape, Riesling, are not yet bearing in commercial quantities.

At the Eyrie, David Lett's failing health resulted in son Jason taking over both management and winemaking in 2005. Jason Lett had already started making his own wine, labelled Black Cap, at another winery. When he took over at The Eyrie, he brought Black Cap with him and produced it until 2011. Current red wines from The Eyrie are Pinot noir, Pinot Meunier and Trousseau. Whites are Pinot gris, Pinot blanc, Chardonnay, Muscat Ottonel and Chasselas (vines planted in 2000; a subtle but interesting wine). Production levels are up; in the past, the winery usually produced about eight thousand cases per year, but it is currently producing almost eleven thousand.

The receivers of the Charles Coury Winery asked David Teppola to take over the operation in 1978. Teppola had purchased 240 acres of Yamhill County property in 1974 and planned to build a winery there but decided to take on management of the Coury winery and ultimately purchased it in 1986. He sold wine under both the Laurel Ridge and Reuter Hill labels. Teppola put the property up for sale in 1992 and sold it to Milan Stoyanov. David Teppola continued to lease the property until 2001, when his new winery was ready. Stoyanov subsequently renamed the winery David Hill and started a rehabilitation project. The old and dilapidated farmhouse was renovated and turned into offices and a tasting room. The vineyard, which had been neglected, was cleaned up and Joel Myers brought in as a consultant. (Myers had started at The Eyrie back in the 1980s and now has his own vineyard management firm.) The older plantings of Pinot Noir (Pommard, Wädenswil and "Coury" clones), Pinot blanc, Melon, Chasselas, Muscat, Sylvaner, Semillon, Riesling and Gewürztraminer have been supplemented with Pinot Gris, Chardonnay (Dijon clones 76 and 96) and Pinot noir (Dijon clones 114, 115, 667 and 777). All vines are on their own roots, because the sandy soil in the area discourages phylloxera. The current winemaker is Justin van Zanten, who got his start in Walla Walla Valley during the early 2000s. Mike Kuenz, formerly of Willamette Valley Vineyards, was hired as general manager in 2013. Kuenz is having some of the vines DNA tested; during the author's July 2018 visit, Kuenz stated his belief that the "Coury clone" is actually two different selections.

David Hill is a bit off the beaten path, and the last quarter mile is gravel road, but it's worth the effort to visit, both because of its historical significance and because the wines are pretty good. The winery produces both an oaked and an unoaked Chardonnay, and a side-by-side comparison is revealing.

Dick Erath, whose winery reverted to using only his name after the partnership with Cal Knudsen ended in 1988, sold his winery to Chateau Ste. Michelle in 2006. The Woodinville, Washington winery retained winemaker Gary Horner (hired by Erath in 2003), with the major change being a ramping up of production, going from 75,000 cases per year to 140,000 by 2013. (Most production shifted to another winery, an arrangement that started even before the sale to Ste. Michelle.) A new winery, expected to be completed by 2020, is being constructed at Knight's Gambit vineyard near Dundee. Dick Erath retained ownership of some of his vineyards; in 2017, he sold Prince Hill Vineyard to the Duncan family of California, owners of Silver Oak Winery in Napa Valley.

In 1997, Bill Fuller and his partner sold Tualatin Valley Vineyards to Willamette Valley Vineyards. Fuller was hired by Willamette Valley as a consulting winemaker in 2013.

In 2014, Myron Redford sold Amity Vineyards to Union Wine Company of Sherwood. Redford is now operating a thirty-acre organic farm.

As at The Eyrie, the next generation is running things at Ponzi, Sokol Blosser and Elk Cove. At Ponzi, Anna Maria Ponzi is president, and Luisa Ponzi is winemaker; at Sokol Blosser, siblings Alex and Alison Sokol Blosser are co-presidents, with Alex doubling as winemaker; and at Elk Cove, Adam Campbell is now manager and winemaker.

The next generation has resurrected one winery. Jim Arterberry Maresh, son of the late Fred Arterberry, founded Arterberry Maresh in 2005 and has gone on to produce what some consider to be some of Oregon's finest Pinot noir. Jim Arterberry Maresh is modest about his accomplishments: "All I do is turn great grapes into really good wine."[216]

Another winery started in the early 2000s was Francis Tannahill. A joint venture by spousal team Cheryl Francis (assistant winemaker at Chehalem) and Sam Tannahill (winemaker at Archery Summit), the winery has no vineyards of its own but has been making wine from select vineyards since the 2002 vintage.

Francis and Tannahill were, however just getting started. In 2002, the couple partnered with Bill Hatcher (previously general manager at Domaine Drouhin Oregon) and his wife, Deborah Hatcher (from The Eyrie), to found A to Z Wineworks. The business model for the new company was loosely based on that of a Burgundy *négociant*, that is, a producer that owns vineyards and makes wine but also buys grapes as well as wine made by small producers. The wine from all three sources is often blended, with "Bourgogne" as the only appellation. The owners of A to Z had no plans to purchase wine from small producers, instead negotiating contracts for grapes with vineyard owners all over the state. The goal was to produce good Oregon wine (Pinot noir and gris, Chardonnay, Riesling) and sell it at a more accessible price point. It's been a winning strategy; by 2013, A to Z was the top-producing Oregon winery, at 298,000 cases.[217] By 2017, A to Z was producing 375,000 cases.[218] With the addition of a fifth partner (Gregg Popovich), A to Z was able to purchase Rex Hill winery in 2006, adding to its production capability.

Also starting small and growing big was NW Wine Company, started by Laurent Montalieu in 2003. Montalieu had been winemaker at WillaKenzie Estate during the 1990s and in 2002 started his own winery, Soléna Estate. He was focusing on Pinot noir but was being urged to add Pinot gris. Looking for locations that would provide the additional capacity, he and partner John Niemeyer visited a former Mrs. Smith's Pies facility in McMinnville. It was larger than they needed, but Niemeyer suggested they could start doing contract winemaking. This proved to be a lucrative enterprise, and they soon outgrew the McMinnville plant, building a new one in Dundee. By 2013, NW Wine Company was the fourth-largest producer in the state, making 165,000 cases, 49 percent of which was for clients. Included among the company's own labels is Westmount, a brand priced slightly higher than A to Z's wines.

A winery completely dedicated to contract production is 12th and Maple in Dundee. Apparently started by Precept Wine of Seattle but now under Winemakers LLC of Yakima, Washington, the winery has been operating since 2005. A telephone conversation with Paul Lukas of Winemakers LLC yielded little useful information, such as who conceived the operation. The primary client is Erath; 250,000 cases of Erath's "Oregon" bottling were produced at 12th and Maple in 2017.[219]

Union Wine Company of Sherwood was founded by Ryan Harms in 2005. The company produces a number of lower-priced wines under various labels. Their Underwood brand is best known for being available in cans as well as bottles; the canned wines include Pinot noir, Pinot gris, Riesling, a Rosé and a couple of sparkling wines. Union is another company that's gotten big in a hurry, producing the equivalent of 151,000 cases in 2014.

In The Dalles, we find Copa di Vino (Italian for "cup of wine"), founded by James Martin in 2009. Martin and his wife, Moli, had started a conventional winery, Quenett, in 2003. While visiting France in 2008, Martin encountered wine packaged in plastic cups and, in 2009, launched Copa di Vino. The varieties available—Cabernet Sauvignon, Merlot, Pinot grigio, Chardonnay, Moscato, Riesling and White Zinfandel—suggest that the grapes are sourced from Washington, not Oregon. Popular at venues that prohibit glass containers, the six-ounce cups have sold well, with Copa di Vino selling almost a quarter million gallons in 2017.

Joe Dobbes worked as a winemaker at a number of wineries, ending with Willamette Valley Vineyards, where he acquired management experience as well. In 2002, he launched his own label, Dobbes Family Estate, operating out of Torii Mor in Dundee. In 2005, he leased a facility in Dundee and began contract winemaking as well as launching Wine by Joe, his own offering in the "popular premium" range ($10–$15). Both operations were successful, and within a few years his was one of the highest-producing wineries in the state, producing 176,000 cases in 2014.

The wineries described in the previous six paragraphs are, along with Willamette Valley Vineyards and King Estate, the highest producing in the state. It is, however, important to understand that sales-by-brand is another and entirely different metric when trying to asses a winery's status. For example, Erath sells over 250,000 cases annually of its wine, but nearly all of it is made at 12th and Maple.

These very large (for Oregon) wineries produce a significant percentage of the state's annual wine output but are something of an anomaly. In fact, 70 percent of the state's wineries produce fewer than five thousand cases of wine per year.[220]

A common characteristic of these large wineries is the focus on lower-priced wines. It's a segment of the wine market largely ignored by Oregon winemakers prior to the 21st century. Traditionally, Oregon wineries focused on premium wines, with Pinot noir and Chardonnay selling for over twenty-five dollars per bottle and Pinot gris selling for over eighteen dollars (typical 2018 prices). The lower-priced wines from companies like A to Z are an option for those who want Oregon wine but cannot afford regular purchase of the more expensive labels.

What will probably never be seen are "bottom shelf" Oregon wines, ones priced at less than ten dollars per bottle (known as "value" wines). Grapevines in Oregon, particularly in the Willamette Valley, exhibit what viticulturalists call "excess vigor." Even during a dry summer, deep-rooted vines can find the moisture they need to generate heavy canopies. These can overshadow the grapes, inhibiting ripening and encouraging mold. Even with trellising and training systems designed to minimize the effect, it is still necessary to prune back the canopy several times during the growing season, an effort not required in drier locations such as California. Canopy management is a labor-intensive task, one which drives up the cost of grapes, and is why you'll never see a seven-dollar Willamette Valley Pinot noir.

The success of Oregon wine has attracted major players, but not all have emphasized high production. The Jackson family of California, whose best-known brand is Kendall-Jackson, have acquired four Willamette Valley wineries, these being Gran Moraine, Zena Crown, WillaKenzie and Penner-Ash, and at all of these, quality is emphasized over quantity. Such acquisitions can be advantageous to the original winery owner, who often can stay on as manager or winemaker (as Lynn Penner-Ash has done). Probably the greatest benefit is access to the distribution channels possessed by the parent company.

Distribution is, in fact, the largest challenge faced by Oregon's small-to-medium wineries. Many are increasingly emphasizing direct sales, from the tasting room, via wine clubs and by online sales. Nearly all wineries have websites, and many are configured for eCommerce. Direct sales accounted for 17 percent of overall sales in 2016;[221] the percentage is higher for smaller wineries.

Most wineries also host various events intended to encourage sales and attract new customers. Concerts, winemaker dinners and food-and-wine pairings are all popular (often these are combined). Wineries with scenic appeal frequently host weddings. One unique event is offered by RainSong, a small winery west of Junction City. RainSong offers "Barrel Bottling" parties; a group of customers can get together on a barrel purchase, bottling the wine and labeling the bottles themselves. A BBQ and picnic usually follow.

Some wineries also incorporate another type of business. Youngberg Hill, west of McMinnville, doubles as a bed-and-breakfast, and Ankeny Vineyard's tasting room offers wood-fired pizza.

But for many Oregon wineries, the key to success remains producing the best wine they can make. Establishing a reputation for top-quality wine will create a demand for it and provides leverage when dealing with distributors. (Even so, even these winemakers will tell you that distribution and sales are an ongoing challenge.) There are several dozen Oregon wineries that continue to produce Pinot noir comparable to Burgundy's best, and demand for these is high. There are some, like Shea Vineyards "Homer Block," which rarely even appear on store shelves and don't stay there long when they do.

Not surprisingly, Burgundy's interest in Oregon remains high. Maison Louis Jadot, Drouhin's chief rival, has been producing "Résonance" since the 2013 vintage, and Domaine du Liger-Belair has partnered with Evening Land's Mark Tarlov to create Chapter 24 (which recently acquired Witness Tree winery).

The center of Oregon's wine industry remains the northern Willamette Valley, where Pinot noir now accounts for 74 percent of vineyard acreage[222]

Barrel bottling party at RainSong Vineyard. Owner Mike Fix supervises the operation. *Photo by the author.*

(Pinot gris is a distant second, at 12 percent and Chardonnay is third, with 7 percent). Chardonnay is enjoying a modest resurgence; although the early-ripening Dijon clones became available at the end of the 1980s, it took a while for these to catch on. The loss of diversity is unfortunate, because there are so many cool-climate grapes that do well in Oregon. There is excellent Riesling and Gewürztraminer being made in the Willamette, and Dieter Boehm, owner and winemaker at High Pass Winery west of Junction City, has been making excellent wines from unusual German varieties like Scheurebe and Huxelrebe.

Reduced diversity is not the only vinicultural change since the 1970s. In fact, as pointed out by David Adelsheim in a recent interview, nearly every aspect of grape growing and winemaking has changed since the pioneering days of the 1970s. The growers are using different clones, phylloxera-resistant rootstock, different row and vine spacing, different trellising/training systems and different management and harvesting practices. In the winery, new equipment has been developed that improves and/or automates much of process yet still provides the "gentle touch" that Pinot noir requires, such as destemmers that leave the grapes whole and bladder-type grape presses. Many white wines are now partially or wholly aged in stainless steel instead of oak barrels.

One thing that appears not to have changed is the spirit of cooperation and collaboration that exists between Oregon winemakers. Even the larger operations will assist one another; in a 2007 interview, Jim Bernau described how King Estate provided a replacement when one of Willamette Valley Vineyard's presses failed.[223]

Perhaps the most extraordinary example of this fellowship is the support given to the Brooks family. Jimi Brooks started Brooks Wines in 1998, locating the winery and vineyard in the Eola-Amity hills. Brooks's contemporaries all speak of his dedication to his craft and his infectious enthusiasm. His last night was an enjoyable one, wining and dining with fellow winemakers (including Sam Tannahill and Josh Bergström) at a McMinnville restaurant. The next morning, a Sunday in early September 2004, Brooks suffered a fatal heart attack. He was thirty-eight.

Brooks had been briefly married, with the union producing a son, Pascal, who was born in 1996. Pascal was Jimi Brook's heir, and when Pascal's aunt, Janie Brooks Heuck, arrived after Jimi's death and learned of the impact he'd made on the local winemaking community, she decided to take on management of the winery. Despite having her own family in California, she wanted to both preserve Jimi's legacy and ensure the winery would be a successful business when Pascal came of age. She received support from many area growers and winemakers, who assisted with the 2004 harvest and continued to help over the following years. Jimi's close friend Chris Williams agreed to become the Brooks winemaker and remains so in early 2019. Heuck and Williams have made Brooks Wines a successful enterprise, producing not only good Pinot noir but excellent Riesling as well. Most of these are dry, but the off-dry "Sweet P" is an author favorite. Pascal Brooks graduated from UC Santa Cruz in 2018, and as of this writing, he is in France looking for a job with a Beaujolais winery.

At a more formal level of organization, in 2004 the Yamhill County Wineries Association expanded to become the Willamette Valley Wineries Association. There are now over two hundred member wineries. A goal of many of the members was the establishment of "sub-appellations" within the Willamette Valley AVA. The first to be approved, at the end of 2004, was Yamhill-Carlton, followed by the Dundee Hills, Ribbon Ridge and McMinnville AVAs in 2005. In 2006 the Eola-Amity Hills and the Chehalem Mountains AVAs were approved. There are additional sub-Willamette

AVAs under consideration; the potentially most significant is the Van Duzer Corridor, which is discussed further in the next chapter.

As for the state-level Oregon Wine Advisory Board, this was replaced in 2004 by the Oregon Wine Board. Like its predecessor, it receives funding via the wine grape tax but is now independent of the Oregon Department of Agriculture, with the board members being appointed by the state's governor. Being tax-supported, the OWB cannot fund lobbying efforts, and the Oregon Winegrowers Association continues to fulfill that role. The two organizations are complementary, and though they have different boards of directors, they have a common administrative staff, with Tom Danowski currently serving as CEO for both organizations.

Southern Oregon received its first sub-AVA in 2000, this being the Applegate Valley section of the Rogue Valley. At the northwest end of the valley, Joe Ginet, who'd satisfied his mortgage and sold his cows in 2004, began converting the farm from a dairy to a winery. The process was complete in 2006, the year Plaisance Ranch was bonded. Ginet had planted numerous vines during the 1990s and had started a successful nursery business in 1998; King Estate was a major customer. In addition to the grape varieties he already had, Ginet visited relatives in France and took cuttings from their Mondeusé vines (a grape his grandfather had grown). These were sent to OSU, which put them through its testing and quarantine program and finally released them to Ginet. There are no fewer than forty-two varieties in the Plaisance vineyard, and there are currently eighteen wines being made. Most are varietal bottlings, but there are blends as well. The grapes include Pinot noir, Chardonnay and Tempranillo; Rhone varieties such as Syrah, Mourvèdre, Petite Sirah and Viognier; and the Bordeaux varieties Cabernet Sauvignon, Cabernet Franc, Merlot, Petite Verdot and Carménère. This last variety has not existed in Bordeaux since the phylloxera epidemic and was thought to be extinct, but a few years ago some peculiar-tasting Merlot growing in Chile was subjected to DNA testing and revealed to be Carménère. A similar find occurred in Italy with some vines thought to be Cabernet Franc. Today, there are plantings in southern Oregon, in the Washington portion of the Walla Walla Valley and in California.

The author stopped at Plaisance Ranch during his August 2018 visit to the area, and was impressed by the wines. He'd set a limit on how much wine to buy during this trip, and had Plaisance been the first stop, the limit might have been reached with only wines purchased there. As it was, it was the last stop, and after much deliberation, he bought a bottle of Viognier (which his wife loved) and a 2013 Carménère.

Tasting room at Cowhorn Winery, Applegate Valley. *Photo by the author.*

Another Applegate winery of note is Cowhorn. Started by Californians Barbara and Bill Steele in 2002, the vineyard is planted with the Rhone varieties Syrah, Grenache, Viognier, Marsanne and Roussanne. Visiting the tasting room (which has a spectacular view), the author found the wines to be very good and bought a bottle of the 2014 "Syrah 8."

Not in the Applegate but on the north side of Jacksonville is Quady North, founded in 2005 by Herbert Quady, son of California dessert wine specialist Andrew Quady. The vineyard is planted with mostly Rhone and Bordeaux varieties, and the winery has established a reputation for some of the best rosé wines made in Oregon.

The most successful winery and vineyard in the Rogue is Del Rio. Started by Californians Robert and Jolee Wallace in the late 1990s, the winery is the largest in southern Oregon, producing 133,300 cases of wine in 2014. The Del Rio vineyards also supply grapes to over twenty other wineries.

To the north, in the Umpqua Valley, Abacela remains the preeminent winery. HillCrest, Henry and Girardet are all still operating, and another thirty or so wineries have been started in the area. Girardet recently introduced a varietal bottling of Cayuga; this has proven to be immensely popular and sells out every year.

Douglas and Jackson Counties were combined into the Southern Oregon AVA in 2004. (The Rogue and Umpqua AVAs continue as distinct entities.) The "super-AVA" was created to facilitate promotion of southern Oregon wine, with the Southern Oregon Wineries Association doing the actual promotion and PR activities. There are over 150 wineries in the area, with some seventy varieties of grapes. Although SOWA likes to emphasize the diversity of grapes grown in the region, Pinot noir accounts for 53 percent of the acreage.[224] Most of the area is unsuitable for Pinot, but the temptation to jump on the Oregon Pinot noir bandwagon is too irresistible for many growers. Much of Southern Oregon's Pinot noir ends up in "Oregon" appellation wines made by wineries like Erath and A to Z.

Along the Columbia River, the Columbia Gorge AVA was approved in 2004. The forty-mile-long AVA is shared between Oregon and Washington, and there are only 161 acres of vines on the Oregon side. The climate changes dramatically over the length of the gorge, with thirty-six inches of rain per year at the western end and only nine at the eastern end.

The Dalles sits right at the boundary of the Columbia Gorge AVA and the Columbia Valley AVA, and the old Mesplie farm straddles the boundary. In 2001, Lonnie Wright was able to purchase the property and launched his own label, The Pines 1852 (that being the year Theodore Mesplie acquired the property). Peter Rosback of Sineann Winery agreed to make the wines; apparently part of the deal was that Sineann would still get some of the grapes from the old Zinfandel vineyard. The Old Vine Zinfandel thus comes in two labels, Sineann and The Pines 1852. Wright also planted Syrah on the property, as well as additional Zinfandel from cuttings taken from the old vines. He sources grapes from other vineyards in the area (many of which he manages) and offers Cabernet Sauvignon, Chardonnay, Gewurztraminer, Merlot, Pinot Gris, Syrah and Zinfandel for sale at his tasting room in Hood River. Visiting the establishment in July 2018, the author liked the Pinot gris enough to buy a bottle, along with a 2016 Old Vine Zinfandel.

The next day was spent clambering around the vineyards with Lonnie Wright, including the old Zinfandel plot. The slope is steep, and that, along with the 103-degree heat, made it a bit of a challenge. Retiring to the Wright residence, a tall glass of cold water preceded the wine. Wright opened two vintages of the Old Vine Zinfandel, along with a bottle of the wine made from the second-generation Zinfandel. All were good, but the 2006 Old Vine was superlative, one of the best Zins the author has ever sampled.

In its annual vineyard and winery census, the SOU research center combines data from the two Columbia AVAs into a "Columbia River and at large" category. The "at large" is the Oregon part of the Snake River AVA (shared with Idaho); fortunately, there are only seventy acres of vines in the Oregon portion of that AVA, and for the purpose of analysis, these can be ignored. Cabernet Sauvignon is the most widely planted grape in the Oregon part of the two Columbia AVAs, at 24 percent, followed by Pinot noir (16 percent), Syrah (14 percent) and Merlot (12 percent). A myriad of other grapes makes up the balance.

OVER THE LAST TWENTY years, many Oregon growers and vintners have made progress in the area of sustainability. Unfortunately, that effort has fragmented into a number of overlapping certifications. Adding to Salmon Safe and LIVE are USDA Certified Organic (King Estate being one of the first, in 2002), LEED (Leadership in Energy and Environmental Design; the first Oregon winery so certified being Sokol Blosser) and Demeter certified Biodynamic (more about this later). Another sustainability effort, the Carbon Neutral Challenge, had its genesis in 2007 legislation intended to reduce greenhouse gas emissions; by January 2009, over thirty Oregon wineries were participating, with most putting in arrays of solar panels. Food Alliance, another certification entity for organic and socially responsible production, was founded in 1997 by OSU, Washington State University and the Washington Department of Agriculture.

In an effort to create an umbrella certification, the Oregon Certified Sustainable Wine came into being in 2009. For a wine to carry the OCSW certification, its source grapes must come from a vineyard that is certified by LIVE, USDA Organic, Demeter Biodynamic or Food Alliance and must be made at a winery that carries at least one of these certifications (LIVE, originally certifying only farming practices, recently added one for wineries, with WillaKenzie being the first Oregon winery receiving the certification).

Biodynamic agriculture has been around for a while, being introduced by the German agronomist Rudolph Steiner in the 1920s. Quoting the Wikipedia article, "It treats soil fertility, plant growth, and livestock care as ecologically interrelated tasks, emphasizing spiritual and mystical perspectives." There is no arguing that many of the organic fertilizer "preparations" used by biodynamic farmers are efficacious, and treating farm acreage as part of a larger ecosystem is certainly a good thing, but much of biodynamic theory and practice is considered by the more scientifically inclined to be just a lot

Many Oregon wineries have installed solar panels as part of the Carbon Neutral Challenge. These are at Tyee Wine Cellars, south of Corvallis. *Photo by the author.*

of hooey. For example, one practice is to stuff a cow horn with manure and ground quartz and then bury it so that it can "harvest cosmic forces in the soil"; the cosmically charged quartz is later added to fertilizer. The reliance on astrology is another attribute that encourages detractors, who like to point out that Rudolph Steiner claimed to have conceived the concept after telepathic consultation with spirits from beyond the material world.

A number of Oregon wineries have gone biodynamic, including King Estate and A to Z, both of which have received a Demeter certification. However, many favor more scientific approaches to sustainable viticulture and wonder if biodynamic certification is, in some cases, acquired to use as a selling point for a certain demographic of wine consumers.

Perhaps more significant is certification as a "B Corporation." Achieving a B Corp certification requires the company to meet not only environmental standards but social ones as well, such as the wages it pays and diversity within the workforce. A to Z was the first winery to receive a B Corp certification, with six more Oregon wineries receiving it by early 2019.

PROBABLY THE MOST NOTABLE marketing initiative in the last twenty years is the Oregon Pinot Camp. The first of these was held in 2000, with forty wineries sponsoring. Members of the wine trade (distributors, retailers, restaurateurs and sommeliers) were invited to a three-day tour of Oregon wine country, which included winery and vineyard visits, wine tastings and meals at various area restaurants. Originally conceived as a one-time event, it's been held every year since, with over fifty wineries currently participating.

Pinot noir sales received a small boost from the movie *Sideways*, released in 2004. Studies show that the increase was as much as 16 percent in some locations.[225] The movie was, however, filmed in California wine country, and it probably did more for sales of California Pinot than for Oregon.

On the research and education front, in 2004 Chemeketa Community College in Salem instituted a viniculture program. Impressed by the "hands on" approach, Barney Watson left OSU to take a position as instructor with the Chemeketa program. At OSU, the Oregon Wine Research Institute was created in 2008; the institute's goal is to improve collaboration between university researchers and the USDA. The university currently has one full-time professor of viticulture (Patricia Skinkis) and two in enology (James Osbourne and Elizabeth Tomasino).

Covering all of this was Hopkins and Cohen's *Oregon Wine Magazine*, which changed its name to the one currently used (*Oregon Wine Press*) in 2004. Hopkins and Cohen decided to retire in 2006, selling the publication to the *McMinnville News-Register*. Hillary Berg was hired as managing editor and is still working in that capacity as of March 2019.

THE GROWTH OF THE Oregon wine industry over the last fifty years is nothing short of phenomenal. From a handful of *vinifera* winegrowers and a few dozen acres of vines, it has grown into one of the state's major industries. There are hundreds of wineries and tens of thousands of acres of vines, contributing over $3 billion per year to the state's economy and employing over seventeen thousand people.[226] The Willamette Valley has proven to be an optimum location for Pinot noir, and its wineries have established themselves as a preeminent source of wine from that grape.

The downside of this is that the Willamette's vineyards have become something of a monoculture, with three quarters of the grapes being Pinot noir. It's a lot of eggs to have in one basket, and anything that can disrupt the production of high-quality Pinot will have a dramatic effect on the industry.

15

ARMAGEDDON?

Selected entries from David Lett's journal, 1965:

20th July – Light showers night of 19th and through the day.
11th August – Heavy rains in Silverton. Lt. through 14th Aug.
19th August – Lt rain through 23rd Aug
25th Sept – Light frost last week.

For anyone not practicing politically motivated self-deception, it's obvious that today's climate is dramatically different from thirty years ago or even ten years ago. When the author and his wife moved to Oregon at the beginning of 2007, our real estate agent told us that we didn't need a house with central air-conditioning. "You'll want it only two or three days a year" was her advice. We followed our own counsel and held out for that feature, but for the first few years it seemed she was right. Daytime temperatures rarely exceeded ninety degrees during the summer months, and one could count on a light shower every few weeks.

That hasn't been true for a while now.

The modern pioneers of viticulture in Oregon, Charles Coury and David Lett, understood the region's climate was optimum for Burgundian varieties such as Pinot noir, because, in an average year, the growing season was just long enough for the grapes to mature. This "just long enough" matching makes for superior grapes, and without those, winemaker Lett, with only six years of experience, could not have made a wine that matched Burgundy's best. "The wine is made in the vineyard," has been the mantra of Oregon winemakers ever since.

The match of Willamette climate and Pinot growing season has existed for a long time, but that relationship is coming to an end. The climate in the valley is now marked by milder winters, earlier springs, hotter, drier summers and warmer autumns. If the theories of Coury and Lett are correct, the grapes will show a decrease in quality.

In his 1964 master's thesis, Coury cites data showing that in Burgundy, Pinot noir requires 2,260 "heat units" (today known as "growing degree days") to mature. This requirement goes up as one goes south, because the length of the summer day becomes shorter. Burgundy straddles the 47th parallel, while the Willamette straddles the 45th, so the degree day requirement in the Willamette is about 2,300. Site selection, such as on a south-facing slope, can reduce the requirement.

As can be seen in the accompanying graph, in the last few years, the GDD for the northern Willamette has exceeded 2,300—in some years by quite a bit. There is also a clear upward trend, which has been true for a while. Graphs presented by Dr. Gregory Jones (formerly at Southern Oregon University, now at Linfield College) show a steady increase since the 1950s.[227]

Of course, there is more to it than simple heat summation (which is what GDD measures). A saving grace for several recent vintages has been the fact that Oregon has an autumn. Even if there have been summer heat waves, the cooler days of September generally bring the grapes back into balance. An exception was 2014, when warm temperatures extended into autumn. Most of September's daily temperatures were higher than average, with ninety-seven degrees recorded at McMinnville on September 6 and ninety-five degrees on the twentieth. The first week of October saw temperatures in the mid-to-high eighties. Many wineries managed to make good wine anyway, a testament to their winemakers' skills.

In addition to unbalanced grapes (too much sugar and too little acid), Dr. Jones has identified a number of other issues associated with climate change. One is an increase in climate variability; though the average temperature will increase, there are more frequent temperature anomalies. (The extremely hot year 2014 in fact started with a record snowfall.) Another is altered disease/pest timing and severity and the distinct possibility that there will be new insect pests which previously could not tolerate an Oregon winter. Water availability will also be an issue; reduced rainfall may require the introduction of irrigation, particularly for young vines. There are also unknowns, such as the direct effect on grapes of increased atmospheric carbon dioxide.

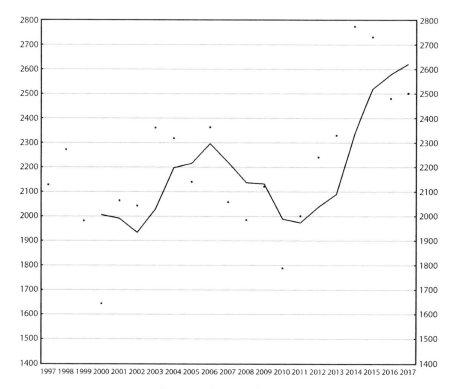

Growing Degree Days
McMinnville Oregon
April 1 - October 31
Solid line is four year moving average

Heat summation data for 1997–2017. *Graph by the author.*

A secondary effect is smoke from wildfires, on the increase because of the hotter, drier climate. The year 2017 saw the Willamette fill with smoke during late August and early September. There was less in 2018, but the Rogue Valley was hard hit, and California wineries canceled grape orders with southern Oregon growers, citing concerns about smoke taint.

There are a number of mitigating techniques and strategies available. One is to use clones and rootstocks that create a vine with a longer growing season. Another approach is to use trellising and training systems that alter the canopy to create more shade; changes in row orientation and spacing can supplement this approach.

Moving the vineyards themselves is an extreme option but will probably be necessary. Shifting them to east-facing slopes and to higher altitudes will help, as will planting in cooler regions. One such location is the Van Duzer corridor, a gap in the coast range west of Salem. Cool ocean breezes reduce the temperatures in the corridor and the Eola-Amity Hills at its eastern terminus, particularly at night. The breeze also dissipates some of the haze from wildfires. In the past, some of the corridor's western vineyards in fact had problems with ripening; Dave Masciorini, owner of Namasté Vineyards, has told the author that the recent warm years have eased his ripening concerns.

Vineyard acreage in the corridor and the adjacent hills is on the increase. Several years ago, Domaine Drouhin Oregon acquired the Roserock vineyard in the Eola-Amity Hills. On a recent visit to DDO, the author compared the 2016 Roserock Chardonnay to the 2016 Dundee-sourced "Arthur." The Roserock had a crisp, clean character that made it the purchase choice.

A paper presented by Dr. Jones in 2007 includes a map showing projected growing regions in 2049.[228] The version that assumes a high rate of climate change (the more probable one, considering the current political climate) shows most of the Willamette Valley becoming Region II, with a Region I zone located in the foothills of the coast range and the Cascades. The pattern of viticulture will likely be Burgundian and Alsatian varietals in the foothills, and Bordeaux, Rhone and Spanish varieties in the Valley.

So, if you're a fan of Dundee Hills Pinot noir, well…enjoy it while it lasts.

16

THE OREGONIAN, PART II

H is friend drove him there, helping him out of the car when they arrived. They were meeting the new owners of the property, a wealthy family from Portland. He told them about his years planting and tending the vineyard, the long, exhausting days. He told them about frosts, about pests, about birds stripping vines bare in a matter of hours. He told them about good vintages and bad. He told his story quietly, but with the pride of accomplishment.

He told them about finding the vine, the relic Pinot Meunier vine, near the top of the butte. He pointed to its descendants, the two vines at either end of the deck. Intrigued, one of the new owner's daughters researched the property's history and discovered the French family who first owned it, who planted the vine.

As he left, he took a last look at the vineyard…and remembered.

JACK PARKER MYERS DIED two weeks later, on July 28, 2001. His ashes were spread over Neahkahnie Mountain, a favorite place. A gathering was held soon after, at Cliff Anderson's winery. People spoke, recalling stories about him. Myron Redford told of the incident with the Cat D2. Dick Erath told of the overripe Pinot noir and the dessert wine made from it. Others had their own stories to tell. They lifted glasses of Oregon wine and toasted his accomplishments, his life and his legacy.

Champoeg Wine Cellars, July 14, 2001. From left to right are Ted Ottmar, Cliff Anderson and Jack Myers. *Courtesy of Brenda Eggert and Champoeg Wine Cellars.*

17
THE VINE, PART III

The vine is gone, but its grandchildren still stand at either end of the deck outside the winery's tasting room. It exists nowhere else. The author hopes to obtain rootings in the near future; there is phylloxera in the vineyard, and it's just a matter of time before it reaches the Meunier vines.

The vine lives. For now.

NOTES

Chapter 2

1. Wagner, *American Wines*, 47.
2. McLoughlin, *Letters of John McLoughlin*, 79.
3. Farnham, *Farnham's Travels*, 66.
4. Erigero, *Fort Vancouver Cultural Landscape Report*, 1,824–28, Site, Garden and Orchard, Seeds.
5. Allan, "Reminiscences of Fort Vancouver," 76.
6. Erigero, *Fort Vancouver Cultural Landscape Report*, 1829–46, Transition, Site, Garden, Location, Size and Boundaries.
7. Whitman, *Diaries and Letters*, loc. 668, Kindle edition.
8. Cardwell, "First Fruits II," 155.
9. Lee and Frost, *Ten Years in Oregon*, 140–42.
10. *History of the Pacific Northwest*, 214.
11. Cardwell, "First Fruits I," 36.
12. California State Agricultural Society, *Transactions of the California State Agricultural Society, 1859*, 198.

Chapter 3

13. Wine-Searcher, "IGP Franche-Comte Wine," https://www.wine-searcher.com/regions-igp+franche-comte.
14. Mathiot, *History of the Mathiot Family*, 3.

15. Ibid., 17.
16. California State Agricultural Society, *Transactions of the California State Agricultural Society, 1858*, 258.
17. Sullivan, *Companion to California Wine*, 7.
18. Haeger, *North American Pinot Joir*, 34–35.
19. Shipley, "Grapes in Oregon in 1869," 75.
20. Sullivan, *Companion to California Wine*, 214.
21. Ibid.
22. *Federal Cases*, Book 26, 1197–200.
23. U.S. Census, 1880, agricultural schedule, Oregon, Marion County, Butteville district.
24. McMurtrie, *Statistics of Grape Culture*, 5.
25. Gillenwater, personal communication with author, 28 February, 2018.
26. McMurtie, *Statistics of Grape Culture*, 31.
27. Oregon Board of Horticulture, "Report of Commissioner," 37.
28. Mathiot, personal communication with author, February 10, 2018.

Chapter 4

29. Brown, "Wine in the Rogue Valley—Peter Britt and the Beginnings" [hereafter "Beginnings"], 5.
30. Ibid, 7.
31. Oregon Travel Information Bureau. "Britt Sequoia," https://ortravelexperience.com/oregon-heritage-trees/britt-sequoia.
32. Brown, "Beginnings," 9.
33. Daspit, "In Search," 9.
34. Brown, "Beginnings," 10.
35. Ibid.
36. U.S. Census, 1880, agricultural schedule, Oregon, Jackson County, 1–25, 1–2.
37. Southern Oregon State Board of Agriculture, *Resources of Southern Oregon*, 51.
38. Ibid., 53.
39. "Making of Wine in the Chehalem Hills of Oregon," *The Sunday Oregonian*.
40. U.S. Census, 1900, agricultural report, 675.
41. Plaisance Ranch, "Plaisance History."
42. Brown, "Wine in the Rogue Valley: From Peter Britt to Rebirth" [hereafter "From Peter Britt"], 16.
43. "Get Silver Medals," *Morning Oregonian*.

44. Neiderheiser, *Jesse Applegate*, 281.

45. Ibid., 284.

46. Purser and Allen, *Winemakers of the Pacific Northwest*, 154.

47. Port of Philadelphia, "Passenger List."

48. Purser and Allen, *Winemakers of the Pacific Northwest*, 154.

49. *Federal Cases*, Book 26, 1197–200.

50. Cardwell, "First Fruits I," 31.

51. Shipley, "Grape Growing," 266.

52. Cardwell, "First Fruits I," 31.

53. Shipley, "Grape Growing," 262.

54. "Grapes," *Willamette Farmer*.

55. Lake, Coolidge, Broetje and Newell, *Grape in Oregon*, 74.

56. Oregon Board of Horticulture, "Report of Commissioner," 37.

57. Lake, Coolidge, Broetje and Newell, *Grape in Oregon*, 79, 68.

58. Stursa, *Distilled in Oregon*, 88–89.

59. Oregon Board of Horticulture, "Report of Commissioner," 37.

60. Lake, Coolidge, Broetje and Newell, *Grape in Oregon*, 79, 84.

61. Stearns, "Grape Growing in this Valley," 244.

62. U.S. Census, 1900.

63. "Viticulture in Willamette Valley," *Morning Oregonian*.

64. Lake, Coolidge, Broetje and Newell, *Grape in Oregon*, 68.

65. "Prizes for Oregon," *Morning Oregonian*.

66. "Get Silver Medals," *Morning Oregonian*.

67. "Making of Wine in the Chehalem Hills of Oregon," *Sunday Oregonian*.

68. Louisiana Purchase Exposition List of Award Winners.

69. Louisiana Purchase Exposition Official Catalogue of Exhibitors.

70. "City and Vicinity," *Oregon City Enterprise*.

71. Wiley, *American Wines*, 7–14.

72. Official Directory of the World's Columbian Exposition, 76.

73. "Making of Wine," *Sunday Oregonian*.

74. U.S. Census, 1900, agricultural report, 675.

75. Malcomb, "Non-Population Census Schedules," 32.

76. "Viticulture in Willamette Valley," *Morning Oregonian*.

77. Helvetia Winery, "History of the Vineyard."

78. Sandoz Farm, "About Us."

79. Leighton, personal communication with author.

80. Vorhees, "Pines Vineyard."

81. U.S. Census, 1900.

82. Roberts, "First Fruit Growers," 3083.

83. Ibid.
84. Roberts, "Fruit Culture in Washington Territory," 229.
85. Hinton, *History of Pacific Northwest Cuisine*, 77.
86. U.S. Census, 1880, agricultural schedule for Umatilla County, Oregon.
87. "Oregon in Japan," *Morning Oregonian*.
88. Sullivan, "Rise and Tragic Fall."
89. U.S. Census, 1900, agricultural report, 611.

Chapter 5

90. "Christian Temperance," *State Rights Democrat*.

Chapter 6

91. "Much Liquor Is Received," *Roseburg News-Review*.
92. Gould, "Portland Italians, 1880–1920," 246.
93. "Italian Factions Are Aroused Again," *Morning Oregonian*.
94. "Federal and State Law in Clash Over Wine Manufacture," *Oregon Daily Journal*.
95. Marsh, *Twenty Years*, 186–87,
96. "Lowe Goes to Jail For Nine Months For Moonshining," *Oregon Daily Journal*.
97. Pinney, *History of Wine in America*, 22.
98. Ibid., 23.
99. Ibid., 19.
100. Ibid.
101. "Old Wine Maker's Product Is Spilled by County Sheriff," *Oregon Daily Journal*.
102. Brown, "From Peter Britt," 16.
103. Wright, interview with author.
104. Leighton, personal communication.
105. Wetherell and Wetherell, "Interview."
106. U.S. Census, 1920, Report for States—With Statistics for Counties, 79.
107. U.S. Census, 1930, Agricultural Report, Vol II, part 3—The Western States, 500.
108. Oregon Historical Society, "Clink! A Taste of Oregon Wine," panel exhibit, panel 3.

Chapter 8

109. Pinney, *History of Wine in America*, 57.
110. Piggly-Wiggly advertisement, *Klamath News*.
111. "For Sale—Miscellaneous," *Capital Journal*.
112. "Hillsboro Winery Makes Grape Market," *Capital Journal*.
113. Advertisement for "Monastery Oregon Fruit Wines," *Eugene Guard*.
114. "Oregon-Made Fruit Wine Now Available Here," *Evening Herald*.
115. Untitled item, *Statesman Journal*, September 14, 1928.
116. Oregon Wine History, "Louis Herboldt."
117. Spreadsheet created by Oregon Wine History Project at Linfield College, extracted from BATF records in 1998.
118. "Licensed Winery Now in Beaver Creek Area," *Corvallis Gazette-Times*.
119. "Secret Method of Winemaking Brings Offers to Hugo Neuman," *Corvallis Gazette-Times*.
120. Purser and Allen, *Winemakers of the Pacific Northwest*, 156–57.
121. "Doerner's Winery at Melrose Being Enlarged," *Roseburg News-Review*.
122. Wetherell and Wetherell, "Interview."
123. "Melrose Wines Still on Market," *Roseburg News-Review*.
124. Oregon City—Park Place Neighborhood—Historical Resources Inventory 1990—Mayer, Samuel, House.
125. "Closing Out Sale," *Capital Journal*.
126. "Local Wine to be Distributed Here," *Eugene Guard*.
127. "Kapphan Winery Makes Progress," *Capital Journal*.
128. Wright, personal communication.
129. Leighton, personal communication.
130. "Wine Made in Salem Finds Broad Market," *Statesman Journal*.
131. "Distillery Uses Oregon Products," *Evening Herald*.
132. "Winery Berries Are Restricted," *Statesman Journal*.
133. "Dutch Mill Loses License," *Capital Journal*.
134. Piggly-Wiggly advertisement, *Medford Mail Tribune*.
135. "Honeywood Winery Celebrates 80 years," *Statesman Journal*.
136. "Wine Made in Salem Finds Broad Market," *Statesman Journal*.
137. "Honeywood Winery Celebrates 80 years," *Statesman Journal*.
138. "Salem-made Wines Are Sold in Distant Parts of Country," *Statesman Journal*.
139. "Wine Laboratory in Oregon Solves Quality Problem," *Medford Mail Tribune*.
140. "Fear Expressed for Oregon's Brewery, Winery," *Bend Bulletin*.
141. "Passed by 1965 Legislature—Liquor," *Statesman Journal*.

Chapter 9

142. Arroyo-Garcia, et al., "Multiple Origins."
143. Bacilieri, et al., "Genetic Structure."
144. Haeger, *North American Pinot Noir*, 18.
145. Pelsy, "Revealed."
146. Ibid.
147. Wikipedia. "Pinot Noir," citing Jancis Robinson (2006).
148. Haeger, *North American Pinot Noir*, 19.
149. Galinié, "Les Graphies Pinot et Pineau," 27.
150. Haeger, *North American Pinot Noir*, 17.
151. Galinié, "Les Graphies Pinot et Pineau," 5.
152. Wikipedia. "List of Grape Varieties."
153. Sullivan, *Companion to California Wine*, 269.
154. Peninou, "History of the San Francisco Viticultural District," 59.
155. Haeger, *North American Pinot Noir*, 35.
156. Hilgard, "Red Burgundy Type," 58.
157. Haeger, *North American Pinot Noir*, 37.
158. Ibid., 46.
159. Nelson-Kluk, "History of Pinot Noir at FPS," 10.
160. Ibid., 9.
161. Brown, "Beginnings," 10.
162. *Oregon Wine Press*, "Golden Opportunity."
163. Wetherell and Wetherell, "Interview."
164. Gaffney, "Umpqua Valley, Oregon."
165. *Oregon Wine Press*, "Golden Opportunity"; Gaffney, "Umpqua Valley, Oregon."
166. Lett, "On Pinot," 1992 speech at UCD.
167. Nelson, "Interview."
168. Coury, "Wine Grape Adaption," 38.
169. Purser and Allen, *Winemakers of the Pacific Northwest*, 163.
170. Lett, "Oregon Wine History Project™ [hereafter OWHP] Interview."

Chapter 10

171. Lett, bank loan application, 1970.
172. Sweet, personal communication with author (email).

173. Lett, "Notes 1965-66," entries for January 1965 and for March 13, 1965.
174. Lett, "Pinot Noir Clones in Oregon," 1–2.
175. Lett, "OWHP Interview."
176. Erath, "OWHP Interview."
177. Lett, bank loan application, 1970.
178. Lett, "30 Year Retrospective"; Lett, "Foundation of Eyrie Vineyards."
179. Haeger, *North American Pinot Noir*, 49.
180. Purser and Allen, *Winemakers of the Pacific Northwest*, 164.
181. "Wine's Doing Fine in the Willamette," *Capital Journal.*
182. Wasserman, personal communication with author (email).
183. Lett, "Emergence of Pinot Gris."
184. Ibid.
185. McCarthy, interview with author.

Chapter 11

186. Erath, "OWHP Interview."
187. Ibid.; Purser and Allen, *Winemakers of the Pacific Northwest*, 155; "Hearing Draws Grape Growers," *Lebanon Express.*
188. Yang, Steele and Hagerstedt. "Analysis of Oregon Grapes for Oregon Wine."
189. Adelsheim, "OWHP Interview."
190. "OSU Researchers OK Five French Wine Grapes," *Corvallis Gazette-Times.*
191. Erath, "OWHP Interview."
192. "Wine Gaining Foreign Flavor," *Statesman Journal.*
193. Sokol Blosser, "OWHP Interview"; Redford, "OWHP Interview."
194. Blosser, personal communication with author (email).
195. Fuller, interview with author.
196. Blosser, personal communication.
197. Myron Redford collection, Linfield Library.
198. Fuller, "Interview."

Chapter 12

199. Erath, interview with author.
200. Redford, interview with author.

Chapter 13

201. Parker, letter to Myron Redford.
202. Sokol Blosser, "OWHP Interview"
203. Government Publishing Office, Electronic Code of Federal Regulations, Title 27, Part 9, Subpart C, Section 9.90.
204. Wagner, "Oregon's Mystery Grape," 14.
205. Ibid.
206. Bernau, "Interview."
207. Linfield College Archives, 1989 Oregon Vineyard Report, 3.
208. Prial, "Pinot Noir Finds a New Home in Oregon Vineyards"
209. Linfield College Archives, 1989 Oregon Vineyard Report, 3.
210. Brown, "Wine in the Rogue Valley: Rebirth 1970–1980," 14–15.
211. Linfield College Archives, 1989 Oregon Vineyard Report, 3.
212. Wright, interview with author.
213. Parker, "1994 Sineann Cellars."
214. Linfield College Archives, 1998 Oregon Vineyard and Winery Report, 10.
215. Rost, "Wine Industry Innovations."

Chapter 14

216. "Vines that Bind," *Register-Guard.*
217. "Big Players Perform," *Oregon Wine Press.*
218. Tannahill, personal communication with author (email).
219. Horner, interview with author.
220. Oregon Wine Board, "Oregon Wine Industry Statistics."
221. Linfield College Archives, 2016 Oregon Vineyard and Winery Census Report, 4.
222. Ibid., 2.
223. Bernau, "Interview."
224. Linfield College Archives, 2016 Oregon Vineyard and Winery Census Report, 4.
225. Cuellar, "Sideways Effect."
226. Oregon Wine Board, "Oregon Wine Industry Statistics."

Chapter 15

227. Jones, "Climate Structure."
228. Jones, "Climate Change," 11.

BIBLIOGRAPHY

Adelsheim, David, "Oregon Wine History Project™ Interview Transcript: David Adelsheim." (2012). Oregon Wine History Transcripts. Transcript. Submission 1. https://digitalcommons.linfield.edu/owh_transcripts.

Allan, George T. "Reminiscences of Fort Vancouver on Columbia River, Oregon, as It Stood in 1832." In *Transactions of the Oregon Pioneer Association, 1881*. Salem, OR: E.M. Waite, 1882.

Arroyo-Garcia, et al. "Multiple Origins of Cultivated Grapevine (*Vitis vinifera L. ssp. sativa*) Based on Chloroplast DNA Polymorphisms." *Molecular Ecology* 15, no. 12 (October 2006): 3707–14.

Bacilieri, et al. "Genetic Structure in Cultivated Grapevines Is Linked to Geography and Human Selection." *BMC Plant Biology* 13, no.1 (2013): 25.

Bend Bulletin. "Fear Expressed for Oregon's Brewery, Winery." March 26, 1963, 5.

Bernau, Jim. "Jim Bernau Interview" (2007). Janis Miglavs Interview Collection. Video File. Submission 20. https://digitalcommons.linfield.edu/owha_miglavs_interviews/20

Blosser, Bill. Personal communication with author (email), October 3, 2018.

Brown, Willard. "Wine in the Rogue Valley: From Peter Britt to Rebirth." Southern Oregon University, 2014. Accessed February 12, 2018. https://digital.sou.edu/digital/collection/p16085coll8/id/432/rec/827.

———. "Wine in the Rogue Valley—Peter Britt and the Beginnings." Southern Oregon University, 2014. Accessed February 12, 2018. https://digital.sou.edu/digital/collection/p16085coll8/id/431/rec/828.

————. "Wine in the Rogue Valley—Rebirth 1970—1980." Southern Oregon University, 2014. Accessed February 12, 2018. https://digital. sou.edu/digital/collection/p16085coll8/id/429/rec/829.

California State Agricultural Society. *Transactions of the California State Agricultural Society, 1858.* Sacramento, CA, 1859.

————. *Transactions of the California State Agricultural Society, 1859.* Sacramento, CA, 1860.

Capital Journal. "Closing Out Sale." October 5, 1937, 11.

————. "Dutch Mill Loses License." October 22, 1942, 12.

————. "For Sale—Miscellaneous." February 21, 1939, 15.

————. "Hillsboro Winery Makes Grape Market." October 19, 1934, 10.

————. "Kapphan Winery Makes Progress." March 7, 1935, 4.

————. "Wine's Doing Fine in the Willamette." November 10, 1972. 13.

Cardwell, J.R. "The First Fruits of the Land. A Brief History of Early Horticulture in Oregon." *Quarterly of the Oregon Historical Society* 7, no. 1 (1906): 28–51.

————. "The First Fruits of the Land. A Brief History of Early Horticulture in Oregon II." *The Quarterly of the Oregon Historical Society* 7, no. 2 (1906): 151–62.

Corvallis Gazette-Times. "Licensed Winery Now in Beaver Creek Area." November 16, 1934, 2.

————. "OSU Researchers OK Five French Wine Grapes." March 21, 1977.

————. "Secret Method of Winemaking Brings Offers to Hugo Neuman." October 10, 1951, 6.

Coury, Charles J. "Wine Grape Adaption in the Napa Valley, California." Master's thesis, University of California at Davis, 1964.

Cuellar, Steven S. "The Sideways Effect." *Wines and Vines* (San Rafael, CA), January 2009.

Daspit, M.J. "In Search of Peter Britt's Original Valley View Vineyard." *Southern Oregon Wine Scene* (Spring 2018): 8–9.

Erath, Dick. Interview with author. September 26, 2018.

————. "Oregon Wine History Project™ Interview Transcript: Dick Erath." (2012). Oregon Wine History Transcripts. Transcript. Submission 2. https://digitalcommons.linfield.edu/owh_transcripts/2

Erigero, Patricia C. *Fort Vancouver Cultural Landscape Report.* Vol. 2. Seattle, WA: National Park Service, 1992. https://www.nps.gov/parkhistory/online_ books/fova/clr/clr2-1c.htm and https://www.nps.gov/parkhistory/ online_books/fova/clr/clr2-2c3c.htm.

Eugene Guard. Advertisement for "Monastery Fruit Wines." April 21, 1937, 4.

―――. "Local Wine to be Distributed Here." November 22, 1936, 4.

Evening Herald. "Distillery Uses Oregon Products." November 24, 1938, 6.

―――. "Oregon-Made Fruit Wine Now Available Here." February 16, 1938, 10.

Farnham, Thomas. *Farnham's Travels, Vol 96.* Bedford, MA: Applewood Books. Originally published 1843.

The Federal Cases, Book 26. St. Paul, MN: West Publishing Company, 1896.

Fuller, Bill. "Bill Fuller Interview." (2015). Browse All Willamette Valley Oral History Interviews. Video File. Submission 26. https://digitalcommons. linfield.edu/owha_willamette_interviews/26.

―――. Interview with author. October 3, 2018.

Gaffney, William. "Umpqua Valley, Oregon." Prince of Pinot. Accessed November 14, 2018. http://www.princeofpinot.com/article/1091.

Galinié, Henri. "Les Graphies Pinot et Pineau (1375–1901)." HAL. Accessed November 14, 2018. https://halshs.archives-ouvertes.fr/ halshs-01215908.

Gillenwater, Helen. Personal communication with author (email). February 28, 2018.

Gould, Charles F. "Portland Italians, 1880–1920." *Oregon Historical Quarterly* 77 (September 1976): 239–60.

Government Publishing Office. Electronic Code of Federal Regulations, Title 27, Part 9, Subpart C, Section 9.90. https://www.ecfr.gov/cgi-bin/ text-idx?c=ecfr&SID=9cfdb16bbeb8c115d87f38c0bc52e68c&rgn=div8 &view=text&node=27:1.0.1.1.7.3.41.70&idno=27.

Haeger, John Winthrop. *North American Pinot Noir.* Berkeley: University of California Press, 2004.

Helvetia Winery. "History of the Vineyard." https://helvetiawinery.com/ history.

Hilgard, Eugene W. "Red Burgundy Type." *Report of the Viticultural Work During the Seasons 1887–1893.* Berkeley: University of California College of Agriculture, 1896.

Hinton, Mark. *A History of Pacific Northwest Cuisine.* Charleston, SC: The History Press, 2013.

History of the Pacific Northwest. Portland, OR: North Pacific History Company, 1889.

Horner, Gary. Interview with author, October 31, 2018.

Jones, Gregory V. "Climate Change: Observations, Projections and General Implications for Viticulture and Wine Production." Paper presented at Climate and Viticulture Congress sponsored by the International Organization of Vine and Wine (OIV) in Zaragoza, Spain, April 10–14, 2007.

————. "Climate Structure, Phenology, and Change in Pinot Noir Wine Regions." Paper presented at ASEV Joint Burgundy-California-Oregon Symposium, June 16–17, 2008, Portland, Oregon.

Klamath News. Piggly-Wiggly advertisement. October 26, 1935, 3.

Lake, Edward R., D.W. Coolidge, John F. Brotje and Wilbur K. Newell. "The Grape in Oregon." *Oregon Agricultural Experiment Station Bulletin*, no. 66 (June 1901). Corvallis, OR: Oregon Agricultural College Printing Office.

Lebanon Express. "Hearing Draws Grape Growers." September 10, 1969, 12.

Lee, D., and J.H. Frost. *Ten Years in Oregon.* New York: self-published, 1844.

Leighton, Mary. Personal communication with author (email). August 3, 2018.

Lett, David. "The Emergence of Pinot Gris." 1992 speech at Wine Tech, Eyrie Vineyards, https://eyrievineyards.com/pdfs/words/January%20 1992%20Wine%20Tech%20Speech.pdf.

————. "Foundation of Eyrie Vineyards." 1992 speech, Eyrie Vineyards, https://eyrievineyards.com/pdfs/words/May%201992,%20 Portland%20Vascular%20Group%20speech.pdf.

————. "Notes 1965–66." Courtesy Jason Lett.

————. "On Pinot," 1992 speech at UCD, Eyrie Vineyards, https:// eyrievineyards.com/pdfs/words/April%201992,%20UCD%20Speech. pdf.

————. Supporting documentation for bank loan application, 1970. Courtesy Jason Lett.

————. "30 Year Retrospective." 1996 speech. Eyrie Vineyards, https:// eyrievineyards.com/pdfs/words/March%201996,%20McMinnville%20 Chamber%20Speech.pdf

Lett, Diana. "Oregon Wine History Project™ Interview Transcript: Diana Lett." (2012). Oregon Wine History Transcripts. Transcript. Submission 3. https://digitalcommons.linfield.edu/owh_transcripts/3.

Lett, Jason. "Pinot Noir Clones in Oregon—A History." Eyrie Vineyards, https://eyrievineyards.com/pdfs/words/Pinot%20noir%20Clones%20 2004.pdf.

Linfield College Archives. "Oregon Vineyard Report—1989." Oregon Wine History Archives. https://oregonwinehistoryarchive.org/regions/ oregon-collection/oregon-vineyard-and-winery-report.

———. Oregon Vineyard and Winery Report—1998." Oregon Wine History Archives. https://oregonwinehistoryarchive.org/regions/oregon-collection/oregon-vineyard-and-winery-report.

———. "Oregon Vineyard and Winery Census Report—2016." Oregon Wine History Archives. https://oregonwinehistoryarchive.org/regions/oregon-collection/oregon-vineyard-and-winery-report.

Louisiana Purchase Exposition, List of award winners, Group 92 (Wines and Brandies), Department of Agriculture, Louisiana Purchase Exposition Records, Missouri Historical Society Archives, St. Louis.

Louisiana Purchase Exposition Official Catalogue of Exhibitors—Department H—Agriculture, 130. St. Louis, MO: Official Catalogue Company, 1904.

Mail Tribune. Piggly-Wiggly advertisement. April 18, 1946, 11.

———. "Wine Laboratory in Salem Solves Quality Problem." June 7, 1940, 9.

Malcomb, Louis. "Non-Population Census Schedules: Description, Accessibility and Disposition." *Indiana Libraries* 11, nos. 1 and 2 (1992): 23–34.

Marsh, Floyd. *Twenty Years a Soldier of Fortune.* Portland, OR: Binford & Mort, 1976.

Mathiot, Kent. Personal communication with author (telephone), February 10, 2018.

Mathiot, Pierre. *History of the Mathiot Family.* Unpublished manuscript: 1891. Accessed November 12, 2018. http://freepages.rootsweb.com/~larry7912/genealogy/Bio/pierre-emile-mathiot.htm.

McCarthy, Steve. Interview with author, 2016.

McLouglin, John. *The Letters of John McLoughlin from Fort Vancouver to the Governor and Committee: First Series, 1825–38.* Toronto, ON: Champlain Society for the Hudson's Bay Record Society, 1941.

McMurtrie, William. *Statistics of Grape Culture and Wine Production in the United States.* Washington, D.C.: Government Printing Office, 1881.

Morning Oregonian. "Get Silver Medals." November 3, 1905, 10.

———. "Italian Factions Are Aroused Again." July 3, 1917, 2.

———. "Portland in Japan." January 6, 1903, 12.

———. "Prizes for Oregon." October 25, 1904, 4.

———. "Viticulture in Willamette Valley." January 1, 1908, 15.

Neiderheiser, Leta Lovelace. *Jesse Applegate: A Dialogue with Destiny.* Mustang, OK: Tate Publishing & Enterprises, 2010.

Nelson, Bill. "Bill Nelson Interview." (2013). *Oral History Interview: Bill Nelson.* Video File. Submission 1. https://digitalcommons.linfield.edu/owha_nelson_interview/1.

Nelson-Kluk, Susan. "History of Pinot Noir at FPS." *FPS Grape Program Newsletter* (October 2003): 9–13.

The Official Directory of the World's Columbian Exposition. Chicago: W.B. Conkey Company, 1893

Oregon Board of Horticulture. "Report of Commissioner, Second District." *Second Biennial Report.* Salem, OR: State Printing Office, 1893.

Oregon City Enterprise. "City and Vicinity." December 21, 1906.

Oregon City—Park Place Neighborhood—Historical Resources Inventory 1990—Mayer, Samuel, House. Accessed November 14, 2018. https://www.orcity.org/planning/13286-s-clackamas-river-drive-samuel-mayer-house.

Oregon Daily Journal. "Federal and State Law in Clash Over Wine Manufacture." October 7, 1916, 13.

———. "Lowe Goes to Jail for Nine Months for Moonshining." December 29, 1921, 3.

———. "Old Wine Maker's Product Is Spilled by County Sheriff." April 17, 1917, 11.

Oregon Historical Society. "Clink! A Taste of Oregon Wine." Panel exhibit, 2014.

Oregon Travel Information Bureau. "Britt Sequoia." Oregon Travel Experience. https://ortravelexperience.com/oregon-heritage-trees/britt-sequoia.

Oregon Wine Board. "Oregon Wine Industry Statistics." https://trade.oregonwine.org/intro/oregon-wine-industry-statistics.

Oregon Wine History. "Louis Herboldt." http://www.oregonwinehistory.com/HistoricalWineries/LouisHerboldt.html.

Oregon Wine Press. "Big Players Perform." *2014 Oregon Wine Almanac.* http://www.oregonwinepress.com/pub/doc/ProductionChart.pdf.

———. "Golden Opportunity." August 2017, 16–17.

Parker, Robert. Letter to Myron Redford. Redford Ccollection, OWHA, Nicholson Library, Linfield College, McMinnville, Oregon.

———. "1994 Sineann Cellars—Zinfandel Old Vine Pines Vineyard." *Wine Advocate*, no. 105, June 29, 1996.

Pelsy, Frédérique. "Revealed: Why Your Pinot Noir Is Actually a Pinot Blanc (Or Was that a Pinot Gris?)." *The Conversation.* 2015. https://theconversation.com/revealed-why-your-pinot-noir-is-actually-a-pinot-blanc-or-was-that-a-pinot-gris-39715.

Peninou, Ernest P. "A History of the San Francisco Viticultural District." Unpublished manuscript. 1965, 1995, 2000. Accessed November 14, 2018. http://www.waywardtendrils.com/pdfs/san_francisco.pdf.

Pinney, Thomas. *A History of Wine in America, II.* Berkeley: University of California Press, 2005.

Plaisance Ranch. "Plaisance History." http://www.plaisanceranch.com/page3/page3.html.

Port of Philadelphia. "Passenger List of Steamship British King. December 12, 1887." Ancestry. Accessed November 13, 2018. https://www.ancestry.com/interactive/8769/PAT840_10-0292/940241.

Prial, Frank. "Pinot Noir Finds a New Home in Oregon Vineyards." Syndicated column, July 6, 1988.

Purser, J. Elizabeth, and Lawrence J. Allen. *The Winemakers of the Pacific Northwest.* Vashon Island, WA: Harbor House Publishing, 1977.

Redford, Myron. Collection at OWHA, Nicholson Library, Linfield College, McMinnville, Oregon.

———. Interview with author. September 27, 2018.

———. "Oregon Wine History Project™ Interview Transcript: Myron Redford." (2012). Oregon Wine History Transcripts. Transcript. Submission 4. https://digitalcommons.linfield.edu/owh_transcripts/4.

Register-Guard. "The Vines that Bind." October 30, 2013, D1.

Roberts, Alvin. "First Fruit Growers of the Pacific Northwest." *Up-to-the-Times* 5, no. 1 (November 1910).

———. "Fruit Culture in Washington Territory." *Tilton's Journal of Horticulture and Florist's Companion* 9 (1871).

Roseburg News-Review. "Doerner's Winery at Melrose Being Enlarged." August 25, 1941, 2.

———. "Melrose Wines Still on Market." February 27, 1961, 60.

———. "Much Liquor Is Received." January 19, 1917, 4.

Rost, Bob. "Wine Industry Innovations Look Promising for the State's Economy and Environment." OSU College of Agricultural Science. http://oregonprogress.oregonstate.edu/winterspring-2002/juiced.

Sandoz Farm. "About Us." http://sandozfarm.com/about-us.

Shipley, Adam. "Grape Growing in the Willamette Valley." *Second Biennial Report of the Oregon State Board of Horticulture.* Salem, OR: State Printing Office, 1893.

———. "Grapes in Oregon in 1869." *Grape Culturis* 2, no. 8 (1870).

Sokol Blosser, Susan. "Oregon Wine History Project™ Interview Transcript: Susan Sokol Blosser." (2012). Oregon Wine History Transcripts. Transcript. Submission 5. https://digitalcommons.linfield.edu/owh_transcripts/5.

Southern Oregon State Board of Agriculture. *The Resources of Southern Oregon.* Salem, OR: State Printing Office, 1890.

Statesman Journal. "Honeywood Winery Celebrates 80 Years." November 21, 2014. https://www.statesmanjournal.com/story/life/food/victor-panichkul/2014/11/22/honeywood-winery-celebrates-years/70031186.

———. "Passed by 1965 Legislature—Liquor." May 15, 1965, 7.

———. September 14, 1928, 14.

———. "Wine Gaining Foreign Flavor." July 3, 1974, 11.

———. "Wine Made in Salem Finds Broad Market." October 11, 1951, 14.

———. "Winery Berries Are Restricted." August 8, 1942, 6.

States Rights Democrat. "Christian Temperance as Opposed to the Total Abstinence, Advocated by the Women's Christian Temperance Union." August 19, 1881, 1.

Stearns, D.H. "Grape Growing in this Valley." *Fruits and Flowers* 2, no. 6 (June 1892): 244.

Stursa, Scott L. *Distilled in Oregon.* Charleston, SC: The History Press, 2017.

Sullivan, Charles L. *A Companion to California Wines.* Berkeley: University of California Press, 1998.

Sullivan, Jack. "The Rise and Tragic Fall of Sol Blumauer." Those Pre-Pro Whiskey Men!, June 8, 2012. http://pre-prowhiskeymen.blogspot.com/2012/06/rise-and-tragic-fall-of-sol-blumau.html.

Sunday Oregonian. "Making Wine in the Chehalem Hills of Oregon." October 30, 1904. 42.

Sweet, Nancy. (Foundation Plant Services). Personal communication with author (email), January 29, 2018.

Tannahill, Sam. Personal communication with author (email), October 31, 2018.

U.S. Census, 1880. Agricultural Schedules for Jackson County, Oregon.

———. Agricultural Schedules for Marion County, Oregon.

———. Agricultural Schedules for Umatilla County, Oregon.

U.S. Census, 1900. Agricultural Report.

———. Population Schedule for North Forest Grove Precinct.

———. Population Schedule for The Dalles.

U.S. Census, 1920. Report for States—With Statistics for Counties.

U.S. Census, 1930. Agricultural Report, Vol II, part 3.

Vorhees, Kori. "The Pines Vineyard: Century Old Vineyard in the Northwest." *Wine Peeps*, August 16, 2010. http://winepeeps.com/2010/08/16/the-pines-vineyard-century-old-vines-in-the-northwest.

Wagner, Phillip M. *American Wines and How to Make Them.* New York: Alfred A. Knopf, 1933.

———. "Oregon's Mystery Grape." *Wines East*, 1989.

Wasserman, Becky. Personal communications with author (email), August 14, 2018.

Wetherell, Shelley Doerner, and Mike Wetherell. "Shelley Doerner Wetherell and Mike Wetherell Interview." (2013). *Oral History Interview: Doerner-Wetherell.* Video File. Submission 1. https://digitalcommons.linfield.edu/owha_doerner_interview/1.

Whitman, Narcissa. *Diaries and Journals, 1836.* Amazon Kindle edition.

Wikipedia. "List of Grape Varieties." Accessed November 14, 2018. https://en.wikipedia.org/wiki/List_of_grape_varieties#Red_grapes.

———. "Pinot Noir." Accessed November 14, 2018. https://en.wikipedia.org/wiki/Pinot_noir.

Wiley, Harvey W. *American Wines at the Paris Exposition of 1900.* Washington, D.C.: Government Printing Office, 1903.

Willamette Farmer. "Grapes." October 19, 1872, 3.

Wine-Searcher. "IGP Franche-Comte Wine." https://www.wine-searcher.com/regions-igp+franche-comte.

Wright, Lonnie. Interview with author. July 15, 2018.

Yang, Hoya, Wilbert Steele and Harry Lagerstedt. "Analysis of Oregon Grapes for Oregon Wine." Circular of Information 598, September 1959. Agricultural Experiment Station, Oregon State College, Corvallis, Oregon.

INDEX

ABOUT THE AUTHOR

Scott Stursa retired from a thirty-eight-year career in information technology in 2016 and took up writing as a second career, publishing his first book, *Distilled in Oregon*, in 2017. He is currently working on a number of projects, both fiction and nonfiction. He lives in Corvallis, Oregon, with his wife and their two cats.

Visit us at
www.historypress.com